C701162516

D1385725

JESUS AND PETER

Growing in friendship with God

Michael Perham

First published in Great Britain in 2012

Society for Promoting Christian Knowledge
36 Causton Street
London SW1P 4ST
www.spckpublishing.co.uk

British Library Cataloguing-in-Publication Data
A catalogue record for this book is available from the British Library

ISBN 978–0–281–06754–1
eBook ISBN 978–0–281–06755–8

Typeset by Graphicraft Limited, Hong Kong
First printed in Great Britain by MPG Books
Subsequently digitally printed in Great Britain

eBook by Graphicraft Limited, Hong Kong

Produced on paper from sustainable forests

*In gratitude to those
who through their human friendship
have drawn me a little deeper
into friendship with God*

Contents

Introduction

Simon Peter, one of those whom Jesus drew into his company of disciples, has been given any number of titles. For some he is 'the Prince of the Apostles'; for others 'the Big Fisherman'. For me, Peter is, above all else, 'a friend of God'; first, though, he was a friend of Jesus, through whom he discovered what God was like, and even friendship with Jesus was not achieved without pain, failure and tears. I want in this book to explore how that friendship establishes itself, how it develops and transforms Peter. Not only is it a fascinating and beautiful story, but also in telling it I find myself attracted to the teaching of the fourth-century bishop Gregory of Nyssa that 'the one thing truly worthwhile is becoming God's friend'.

I discovered that phrase for the first time in the Church of St Gregory of Nyssa in San Francisco, which has as its stated intention to invite people 'to see God's image in humankind, to sing and dance to Jesus' lead, and to become God's friends'. So I do not want simply to retell a fascinating and beautiful story about a man who lived two thousand years ago, but to discover more deeply for myself, and to share with others, what it might mean today to become, or to become more deeply and truly, a disciple of Jesus and a friend of God. For there is a progression in the relationship between Peter and Jesus that readers of this book may wish to consider in their own spiritual lives. How have I moved from enquirer to follower, or to disciple, or to friend? Where am I on that path?

For me friendship is an absolutely key word in my understanding of God and of what ought to characterize my relationship with God. But I don't think deep, intimate friendship is easily achieved. At least it is not so for me; and nor is it, I suspect, for others. In a way I am content that my friendship with God has a long way to develop, that there is a long way to go before I can truly call myself God's friend, but at least I know the process has begun and I know that it is what I want to be. Of course human friendships help. They give me some clue of what it might be like to have a deep and intimate friendship with God. And I thank God for those friendships, not only for what they are in themselves, but also for the way they point to the friendship of God. It's a mind-blowing thought, of course, that God, the creator of all that is, wants to be my friend, wants me to be God's friend, but I believe that both Christian Scripture and Christian reflection and experience through the centuries affirm that it is so.

One reason why I am drawn to the figure of Simon Peter is because his story seems to exemplify both the desire to become God's friend and some of the stages and struggles on the way. Peter very quickly becomes a disciple, a follower, of Jesus. Peter is also, I think, ready to be a servant. But becoming a friend – that takes him time and several moments of crisis. Indeed, at a certain level, the disciple, follower and servant doesn't seem to me to turn into a friend until Jesus asks him by a lakeside after the resurrection, 'Peter, are you my friend?' In this book I want to explore that journey from follower to friend, both in order to deepen my own understanding of what it means to become God's friend and also in the hope that it may speak into the journey that others are making or wanting to make.

My emphasis is on how, gradually, I can know myself to be God's friend. I suspect that when we talk of 'the friendship of God' we are more often than not celebrating the wonderful truth that God wants to be our friend. It is God's initiative, God's desire, God's yearning even, and that is indeed a wonderful thing. What I am more concerned to explore in this book is how the desire for friendship with God grows in you and in me. It is the human side of this relationship that I want to understand and share more clearly. That is why the reader will look in vain in the early chapters for very much of the language of friendship. Friendship was, for Simon Peter, a long way down the line. So it is likely to be with those who try to follow Jesus today.

The word 'friend' is not without its problems. In our society it is most often used of childhood relationships. At school people have 'best friends' and at times fall out of friendship – 'I'm not your friend any more.' It is worrying that all too often we associate friendship with the early stages of life and not with mature adult life – that sometimes, indeed, we look at adult friendship with suspicion, wondering whether it hides some other kind of relationship. This book is in part a protest against that. Friendship is far too important to be left only to children. Becoming God's friend is an adult vocation too. Aelred of Rievaulx mirrors the words of Gregory of Nyssa when he writes, 'Friendship is a stage bordering upon that perfection which consists in the love and knowledge of God, so that from being a friend of our neighbours, we become the friend of God.'

In relating friendship with God to Peter, we must face the difficulty that there is, in a certain way, no single Simon Peter. The Christian tradition over the centuries has created a Peter of whom are told all the stories in the New Testament that include his name and to whom is ascribed the authorship of letters to the early Christians, also bearing his name. It has put together all this material to create a coherent picture of one of the leaders of the embryo church as Jesus brought it into existence, and as he sent the Holy Spirit to go on shaping it after his return to the Father. But, in reality, there are probably four Peters, perhaps even five. There is Peter as Matthew and Mark portray him. There is a slightly different Peter whom Luke describes in his Gospel and in its sequel, the Acts of the Apostles. There is the Peter of John's Gospel, the stories of which overlap only minimally with those in the other Gospel accounts. There is the Peter of the First Letter of Peter and the Simeon Peter of the Second Letter, two epistles which were probably not the work of the same writer, though the Peter of the Gospel stories may well lie behind their writing.

Of course these are not entirely different people – they are the same man. But we can learn more about that man, and about Christian discipleship, if we try to separate out the approaches of the different writers and to look at Peter with their eyes and insights. We cannot resist, and nor should we, the drawing together of these insights to create a more rounded character, which is what faith has done through the ages, but we should resist going down that path too soon. Instead we should allow each writer to speak with his own voice about Peter and, by implication, about our own desire to be disciples of Jesus and friends of God.

In relation to the two letters in the New Testament that bear the name of Peter, I have in Chapter 9 of this book explored some issues of authorship and recognized that we are almost certainly dealing with authorship by followers of Peter, 'the Petrine circle' as they are sometimes collectively known, rather than the apostle himself. In order, however, to avoid the clumsiness of constant reference to 'the author of 1 Peter' or 'the authors of 2 Peter', I have, in Chapters 9 and 10, used the name 'Peter' to describe the letter writer, fully aware that that is a simplification of complex authorship.

I have also had to make a decision about the use of 'Simon' and 'Peter'. There is no consistency in the New Testament, not least because the writers are not agreed about the moment when Jesus gives Simon the new name Peter. For this reason, from the very first chapter, I have called the subject of the book

'Peter' throughout and only made reference to 'Simon' where the biblical text requires it or where a particular point is being made by the use of either 'Simon' alone or 'Simon Peter'.

I need to acknowledge my debt and gratitude to Mary Gray-Reeves, the Bishop of El Camino Real in California, for her part in the early formation of this book. The key central chapters relating to the events of Holy Week and Easter were written after conversation and correspondence with Mary and without her I would never have started the book. Four chapters began their public life as sermons in four churches of the Diocese of Gloucester, of which I am privileged to be bishop – St Mary Magdalene's, Adlestrop; St Michael's, Guiting Power; Tewkesbury Abbey and Gloucester Cathedral. The greater part of the book was written at Hilfield Friary, the mother house of the Society of St Francis, of which I am Bishop Protector, and I acknowledge gratefully the hospitality of the community there in providing me with quiet and space to write. My thanks also to Robert Seifert for some creative thoughts about John 13, to Rosie Woodall for reading the manuscript and correcting a number of errors, and to Joanna Moriarty and Lauren Zimmerman at SPCK, who have encouraged me and helped to make this a better book than it might have been. My final thanks, of course, is to my wife, Alison, who has been patient with my absences and preoccupations at points when the writing of this book has been my principal focus.

I have tried to be a disciple of Jesus Christ all my life and more recently have been very conscious of a desire to become more truly God's friend. In humility, as one who repeatedly fails as both disciple and friend, I offer this to any, whatever their stage on the Christian journey, whether right at the beginning and hesitant or much further down the track and confident, to whom it might speak.

1

Follow me

How do people come to faith in Jesus? What 'converts' them into Christians, whether in an instant or over a period of time? Though there are other routes too, the three different accounts in the Gospels of how Simon Peter came to be a disciple of Jesus Christ are a fruitful way in to this question. Many of us will recognize ourselves in at least one of the three accounts.

We will begin with Luke's version. A little way into his Gospel, he has told his stories of the birth and childhood of Jesus, of the adult Jesus' baptism in the river and of his temptation in the desert. Jesus has appeared in the synagogue at Capernaum and set out his manifesto in gracious words. He has performed a number of healings, including those of a man with an unclean spirit and of Simon's mother-in-law. The first appearance of the man we later get to call Peter is a passing reference in Luke 4.38. It tells us that Jesus entered Simon's house and rebuked the fever from which his mother-in-law was suffering. Luke writes as if we know who this Simon is, and the passage reads as if Jesus and Peter already know one another. Luke 4 ends with Jesus speaking of the compulsion of his mission: 'I must proclaim the good news of the kingdom of God to the other cities also; for I was sent for this purpose' (4.43).

The scene is set for the call of Peter into a more profound relationship with Jesus. Jesus has come to the lake of Gennesaret and a crowd of people have come to hear him teaching. Jesus recognizes that the most effective way to do his teaching would be from a boat close to the shore on which the people have gathered. There are a number of boats to choose from, for the fishermen are there, washing their nets, and Simon Peter is among them. It is his boat that Jesus chooses. He sits there teaching from the boat, Peter, his boat commandeered, no doubt listening to his every word. With the teaching over, the expectation is that Jesus will return to shore, but no. 'Put out into the deep water and let down your nets for a catch,' says Jesus. Peter is doubtful. They have worked all night and caught nothing. But he is nevertheless obedient to Jesus. Luke tells us that the result was a huge catch of fish, so many that other fishermen were needed to help haul them in. There were so many fish that the boats were beginning to sink. But Luke's interest is chiefly not in the size of the catch, but on its effect on Peter:

> When Simon Peter saw it, he fell down at Jesus' knees, saying, 'Go away from me, Lord, for I am a sinful man!' For he and all who were with him were amazed at the catch of fish that they had taken; and so also were James and John, sons of Zebedee, who were partners with Simon. Then Jesus said to Simon, 'Do not be afraid; from now on you will be catching people.' When they had brought their boats to shore, they left everything and followed him. (Luke 5.8–11)

This is also a story about a group of disciples. At the very least there are James and John, for they are named, and there may have been others. One, perhaps, was Andrew, Peter's brother, for – if the Gospels of Mark and John are right – he was involved when Simon was called. But Luke's intention is that, despite the presence of others, Peter should dominate. It is his call that is being described. For Luke, Peter and Paul are the two giant figures of the apostolic church and each has his moment of calling – perhaps one can say (of Peter as well as of Paul) his moment of conversion: Paul in Acts 9, Peter here in Luke 5. And so the others fade into the background in this encounter between Peter and the one he calls 'Master'.

It would seem that Peter already knew Jesus, as the visit to his house implies. We also find him addressing Jesus as 'Master' before ever the great catch of fish has been brought in; this suggests an existing relationship, perhaps as part of a company that is already coming into existence, even though its members are still living in their homes and going about their daily work. But the event on the lake changes everything. They leave all they have, in a sense all they are, and follow Jesus. At a certain level the initiative is theirs, though it is taken in response to what they have seen. In Luke, there is no invitation from Jesus to 'follow me'. Peter does not come because Jesus challenges him to do so. He comes because of what he sees, and Jesus turns for him from 'Master' into 'Lord' (5.8).

This is a pattern of calling and relationship that we can recognize. Sometimes we belong with a group of people, find ourselves drawn into community, before ever we accept fully what that group or community stands for. We sometimes stay there for a long time, not ready to make a deeper commitment, or struggling to discover where truth lies and what we really believe. That is often a good and fruitful place to be. It may be where Peter was in those early days when he was hospitable to Jesus and was happy to call him 'Master', but nevertheless retained his independence and needed time to think things through. Belonging in some way before having a coherent belief is not wrong. It is the way God sometimes works.

But God's desire for each of us is always that we shall move into a deeper relationship with God through Jesus Christ. Luke shows us how it can happen. We look at the evidence of what God is doing. In Peter's case it was the dramatic catch of fish. In Jesus, Peter saw the power of God at work and he crossed a line into faith. At this stage he could not express what faith meant to him, though he could go as far as calling Jesus 'Lord'. In fact what he initially found himself articulating was not about God, but about himself. Because he recognized in Jesus the goodness and the God who was providing for them generously, he became aware of his own lack of goodness: 'I am a sinful man.' This is very often the response of those who suddenly see the goodness of God, and indeed God's beauty, God's glory and God's love: they are overwhelmed by the sense of their inadequacy and sinfulness. Isaiah was the same. When he had his vision in the temple, he found himself saying, 'Woe is me! I am lost, for I am a man of unclean lips, and I live among a people of unclean lips; yet my eyes have seen the King, the Lord of hosts' (Isaiah 6.5).

The divine response, however, is always to raise up and lead on. In Isaiah's case, God said, 'Whom shall I send and who will go for us?' and Isaiah found himself responding, 'Here am I; send me!' To Peter Jesus says, 'Do not be afraid' – words that echo time and time again through the pages of the New Testament from a God whose love casts out fear – 'from now on you will be catching people'. It is a call to mission. Peter doesn't find the words to reply, but he does what he knows he must do. He leaves everything and follows.

The invitation is always to look around and see the activity of a good and generous God. It will not always be visible in the dramatic and the miraculous. Sometimes it will appear in the patient ministry of a priest, the faithfulness of a congregation, the sheer holiness of a man or a woman, the innocent joyfulness of a child. Yet sometimes it will be evident in something so utterly extraordinary and wonderful that words like 'miracle' seem to fit. And very often, in such moments, there is a sense of meeting with Jesus, sensing his presence, his moulding and shaping the event, and belonging goes deeper as believing becomes part of it. It was like that for Luke's Peter. It is a pattern repeated in people's lives around the world every day.

Very different in a number of ways is the call of Peter in the Gospels according to Mark and Matthew. 'Call' is indeed the word. Peter's response is to Jesus' 'Follow me.' Jesus comes to the Sea of Galilee. He is, as Mark puts it, 'proclaiming the good news of God'. He sees Simon and his brother Andrew going about their daily work. Jesus says to them, 'Follow me and I will make you fish for people.' The response is immediate. They abandon their fishing and follow. Jesus then moves on to another pair of brothers, James and John, who are mending their nets. He calls them too. They leave their father with the hired men on the boat and follow Jesus with the same immediacy as Simon and Andrew (Mark 1.14–18).

Straight away it is important to forget the presuppositions we bring from exploring Luke's account. Luke indicates that Peter knew Jesus before the encounter at the lakeside. Mark gives no evidence that this was so. Here we are in the very first chapter of his Gospel. We have read about John the Baptist, about the baptism of Jesus and, very briefly, about the wilderness experience, and then immediately we find ourselves in this passage. The kingdom of God is proclaimed, repentance called for and disciples summoned. There is nothing to suggest that this is anything other than a first and life-changing meeting.

The invitation is to follow Jesus and to fish for people. Literally it is 'come after me'. In origin such an invitation would be a literal one, for the student walked a few paces behind the teacher, but it came to mean not a literal walking behind, but an intellectual, moral and religious following, an imitation of the teacher's pattern of life. And that is clearly what it came to mean in the life of Peter and the other disciples. It is what following as a disciple means today: being formed, conformed and transformed into the shape and pattern of the master's thinking and living. In Matthew 19.27, Peter himself reminds Jesus that 'we have left everything to follow you' and asks, 'What then will we have?' The answer Jesus gives is that they will have 'twelve thrones judging the twelve tribes of Israel' (Matthew 19.27–28).

They did indeed leave everything to follow him – at once. They left behind their livelihood. Peter and Andrew were poor men. We know this from the style of their fishing. Mark's Peter does not have a boat. He and his brother fish, basically, from the shore, with a net weighted with stones round the outside. When thrown into the water it would have been drawn together at the bottom to catch the fish. These were not men with resources. Fishing was how they made ends meet, yet they forsook their source of income and did so straight away.

The call of James and John, immediately afterwards, gives another insight. These were more affluent men: they possessed a boat, had hired workers, fished by the dragnet method and would harvest a substantial catch. There was a business to leave behind in the hands of Zebedee, their father, and the hired hands. But, if they did not give up their economic security in the same way as Peter and Andrew, they gave up their home and family life – the presence of Zebedee, abandoned in the boat, is a poignant reminder of that. And, if that were true of James and John, it was true of Peter and Andrew. Home and family were left behind. Peter's later claim is a radical one – 'we have left *everything* to follow you'. This is much more than following a few steps behind a rabbi, listening to wise teaching. This is total renunciation of the past.

The call to discipleship is radically different from the following of the rabbis in another way too. It lies in the very fact that it is a call, an imperative, from Jesus. The rabbis did not summon disciples. Would-be disciples sought out teachers they wanted to follow. Thus, in Matthew 8.19, a scribe, wanting to attach himself to Jesus' company, assures him, 'Teacher, I will follow you wherever you go.' But this teacher is different. He does not accept those who choose him. He is the one who chooses. It is unusual. Indeed there is only one parallel story in Scripture of this kind of choosing. It is in 1 Kings 19, where Elijah chooses Elisha to be his disciple. This story was almost certainly in Mark's mind, though there is a vital difference. Elijah sets out to find Elisha, who is ploughing his father's field with 12 yoke of oxen. Elijah passes by him, throwing his mantle over him as a way of calling and claiming him. But Elisha doesn't follow immediately. He needs to go home first to take his leave of his parents. Only after that, and after killing and sacrificing the oxen, does he follow Elijah and become his disciple (1 Kings 19.19–21). There is the same total commitment – Elisha leaves behind his previous life, burns his agricultural equipment and feeds the people with meat from the farm. But there is delay, the need to take leave. The response of Peter and the other fishermen was to follow immediately.

Jesus' invitation to Peter is not simply to follow, radical change as that might be in Peter's life. It is also to allow himself to be, in the old phrase, 'a fisher of men'. He is to fish for people. Both Jesus and Peter will have been aware of ideas about fishing for people in the Hebrew Scriptures, and Jesus is almost certainly drawing on these and giving them a new twist. Rarely is the message in the prophets hopeful when it comes to fishing. Warning and judgement are usually present. Jeremiah speaks of 'sending for many fishermen' who will catch the people and 'repay them for their iniquity' (Jeremiah 16.16–18). Amos warns that 'the Lord God has sworn by his holiness: the time is surely coming upon you when they shall take you away with hooks, even the last of you with fish-hooks' (Amos 4.2). The fisherman in these passages is harmful. He brings retribution. He is not good news.

Yet Mark's Peter is to fish for people and Luke's Peter is to catch them. There is no hint at all that Peter's fishing is to be judgemental or harmful. Certainly he is to join Jesus in calling people to repentance, but his mission is to share good news. By making the fishermen agents of his good news, Jesus is, right at the beginning of his ministry, turning his back on the old world of the prophets with their message of a God who sometimes lost patience with his wayward people. Instead he reveals the God who has a gospel – 'the good news of God', as he expresses it – and soon he will send Peter and the other disciples on a mission to show what that good news can achieve. 'They went out and proclaimed that all should repent. They cast out many demons, and anointed with oil many who were sick and cured them' (Mark 6.12–13). Fishermen have turned into agents of the good news God.

How does Mark understand the call of Peter? Certainly for Mark it is a direct and immediate invitation from Jesus, the kind of invitation often extended by God that feels more like an imperative, issued as it is with a deep desire that we should respond. But, I think, key to Mark is that this invitation comes from Jesus with no prior knowledge on Peter's part. Because we may be tempted to read the passage with Luke in the back of our minds, we might want to imagine that the two already know one another, maybe that Jesus has been to Peter's house. But there is no hint of that in Mark. Instead Jesus walks up to a complete stranger, looks at him – perhaps with the kind of instant loving that is recorded when he looks at the rich young man who comes to him in Mark 10.21 – and says 'Follow me!' The response is immediate, inexplicable and, at a certain level, irresponsible. It is unconditional obedience.

It is inexplicable except for two things, the irresistible attractiveness of the man who issues the invitation and the wonderful grace of God at work in Peter without the necessity of deliberation. Whereas Luke wants us to see the power of mighty deeds to make a disciple, Mark wants us to understand that an encounter with a person, with Jesus, from whom flows the love, generosity and beauty of God, can change us in a single moment and begin a relationship that will grow deeper the longer it exists. It is – it was for Peter – akin to love at first sight. When Jesus calls men and women into discipleship it can be like that. The impulse to respond may not be related to what he has done. It may not result from a deep theological understanding of who he is. It is simply that he has a magnetic pull that draws us to him and makes us want to stay with him, walk with him and become his friend. That is what Mark's Peter felt that day by the Lake of Galilee. He felt it because the grace of God was at work in him, enabling him to see what others were failing to see, that here was a man in whom God was at work, a man who would change his life, a man who was offering him an extraordinary vocation – to catch people for the God of grace.

Like Mark, the writer of John's Gospel places the call of Peter at the beginning of Jesus' ministry, in his first chapter, after the Prologue, in which Jesus is revealed as 'the Word made flesh', and the testimony of John the Baptist that Jesus is 'the Lamb of God who takes away the sin of the world'. Before his ministry can begin and the signs of his glory can be unfolded, Jesus must gather around him a company, who will be his witnesses. John the Baptist sees Jesus walking by and repeats his strange description: 'Look,' he says, 'here is the Lamb of God.' Two of his own disciples hear this. One of them is Andrew, Simon Peter's brother.

Again this idea – that Peter's family were already involved in this new religious movement through Andrew being a disciple of John – is unique to the Fourth Gospel. Andrew and a fellow disciple respond to John's words by going after Jesus – the word used is 'following', and there is an ambiguity about whether it is an echo of the call to 'Follow me' or simply means following to see where Jesus is heading. Perhaps the latter, for when Jesus asks them what they are looking for, they simply ask where he is staying. Jesus invites them to 'come and see' and they remain with him all day. But then we discover why this encounter is so important. Andrew seeks out his brother.

> He first found his brother Simon and said to him, 'We have found the Messiah' (which is translated Anointed). He brought Simon to Jesus, who looked at him and said, 'You are Simon son of John. You are to be called Cephas' (which is translated Peter).
>
> (John 1.41–42)

At first sight, John the Evangelist is giving us a third, very different version of Peter's call. For John he is called through the intervention of his brother. He is Andrew's convert. Were it not that Jesus has something crucial to say to him when they meet, this call into discipleship might seem very low key. Andrew plays the bigger part in the story – Andrew who is always bringing people to Jesus, whether it is his brother, or the young lad with the loaves and fishes when Jesus needs to feed a multitude, or Greeks who want to see Jesus. Nor is the bringing of Peter to Jesus as compelling a story as the one that follows, when Nathanael is spotted by Jesus under the fig tree.

In the course of this story Andrew's understanding of Jesus moves forward over the course of a very few hours. At the beginning of the story he is John the Baptist's disciple; by the end he is following Jesus. When he first meets Jesus he calls him 'Rabbi', but by the end he is declaring Jesus to be the Messiah, the Anointed One. An afternoon with Jesus and his understanding has grown, but still he is falling short of what John has proclaimed, that this is the Lamb of God and the Son of God. It is as Messiah that Jesus is introduced to Peter and Peter to Jesus. Compared with his brother, Peter has some catching up to do.

There follows another of those moments when Jesus looks with perceptive eyes of love and knows the person he is seeing deeply even at first encounter. For he fixes his gaze on Simon, as he has been called, recognizes who he is – 'you are Simon son of John' – and proclaims who he will become – 'you are to be called Cephas (which is translated Peter)': 'Cephas' from the Aramaic *kepha* and Peter from the Greek *petra*, both meaning 'rock'. Peter is to be the rock-man. It is said in the future tense; this is something he will become. And indeed he does, little by little, as his story unfolds. The giving of a new name is, of course, not unique to Peter. Usually it is a sign of God's blessing and an indication that God will be at work in the recipient of the new name. Abram becomes Abraham, Sarai becomes Sarah, Jacob becomes Israel, later Saul will become Paul. Here Simon becomes, or at least begins to become, Peter. For in meeting with Jesus he makes a new beginning and appropriately is given a new name.

In terms of the relationship between Jesus and Peter, the most striking element is Peter's passivity and silence. He takes no initiative. Andrew brings him; Jesus addresses him. Peter says nothing. This is the Peter who in other contexts has much to say: words tumble out, not always the most appropriate ones. Here he is silent. He simply receives a new name. He is not mentioned again in John's Gospel, except for a passing reference as Andrew's brother in John 6.8, until the events leading to the Passion. Clearly he is incorporated into the company of the disciples, but it is almost as if he is struck dumb by his encounter with the one who has looked at him and spoken his names.

Hidden in this little story is a deceit – you might even say a lie. For what Andrew claims is that they have found the Messiah. But, of course, they have found nothing. They have responded to what has been declared to them, clearly spelled out to them, repeated, by John the Baptist. And, at a deeper level, they have been found by Jesus. As in Mark, it is the magnetic pull of the one in whom the glory of God is to be revealed that draws them. Andrew is drawn by Jesus' teaching as they sit through the late afternoon and the evening in the house where he is staying; Peter in the moment Jesus looks upon him and names him afresh. They may not know it, but it is Jesus who is doing the finding and he has found himself disciples who will become his friends.

So what model of calling to discipleship is being shown in the Fourth Gospel? What we are being shown is that many people come to faith and discipleship through the ministry of others. Peter was introduced by Andrew. One person is brought to church by a friend; another is given a challenging book to read by a wise acquaintance. Some are converted by the sheer patient love and goodness of their Christian partner; others are moved in the end by persistent trusting prayer for their conversion on the part of a mother, a friend or a whole community. People are often brought to Christ by another. If people are wise they will bring their acquaintances to Christ gently, allowing them to come at their own speed. It is a way into discipleship, accompanied by someone who cares for us. It is often the way God works.

But that last sentence is important. It is God at work – through human agency, certainly, but it is still God at work. It is not that we find Jesus Christ in those who bring us. Rather, it is that Jesus Christ finds us. And when he finds us we may, like the Peter of Luke's Gospel, fall at his feet, recognize our sinfulness and resolve to accept his call to follow him. Or we may, like the Peter of John's Gospel, say nothing at all, but sense that we are loved, and let ourselves be led, wanting to discover something deeper, something more.

2

A little faith

———————•◦•———————

Peter has started on a journey. He has taken the decision to follow this magnetic Jesus and so his formation as a disciple has begun. We need to follow him now through the eyes of just one of the Gospel writers, Matthew. For it is Matthew who will bring to us three highly significant moments in Peter's deepening understanding of Jesus. They will demonstrate some of the next stages in finding the way into relationship with Jesus. One involves placing oneself under the authority of his teaching. A second involves experiencing a call, even while still very much a learner, to become part of the mission. A third entails being drawn into the generous hospitality Jesus wants to be on offer in the Church. In a fourth we come to the point where it may be right to explore baptism.

What happens next to Peter, now he has been drawn into the little band of followers who keep company with Jesus, is that he receives a great deal of teaching and witnesses some mighty acts of power.

As Matthew tells the story, Jesus has no sooner called the first disciples, Peter among them, than a crowd appears, hungry for his teaching. The teaching he gives in chapters 5–7 has been called by subsequent generations 'the Sermon on the Mount'. Whether it did all come bubbling out of Jesus on a single occasion, as the crowd sat there taking in his every word, or whether – as the other Gospels imply – Matthew has brought together teaching by Jesus that was originally much less systematic and was spread over a number of occasions, is of no great consequence. The fact is that here was a wonderfully articulate, prophetic teacher engaging with every area of life – anger, adultery and alms-giving, oath-taking, enemies and hypocrisy, anxiety, prayer and fasting, and much more – and Peter heard it all. The teaching was not aimed specifically at the disciples, the committed ones who were already following, but at the crowd. No doubt, from within the crowd, there were those who felt sufficiently drawn by the teaching to join the itinerant company. But, whether the teaching was directed at the disciples or not, they were there and they heard it, absorbed it and were formed by it, Peter among them, as he began to find his way into the mind of Jesus.

Hearing and heeding the teaching is an important part of following Jesus. The Church is sometimes wary of making too much of Jesus' ethical teaching, of which there is plenty in the Sermon on the Mount, because the world outside the Church is all too ready to regard Jesus simply as a godly teacher, an exemplar of the moral life. The Church always wants to protest that Jesus is much more than that – that his deepest significance, the thing that makes him a saviour, is not what he said, but what he did, supremely what he did on the cross. Nevertheless, heeding the teaching is an inescapable part of discipleship. It even comes into friendship, perhaps a little surprisingly, when Jesus says that 'you are my friends if you do what I command you' (John 15.14). Being a disciple is much more than being an admirer. The world is full of people who admire Jesus and are inspired by his personality. But following Jesus means listening intently to what he teaches and trying to live the way he advocates, not picking and choosing the parts of his teaching that appeal and jettisoning those that we find difficult or challenging. There has to be a sense that we are coming under his moral authority.

That in itself has some complexity, however. We do not always know when Jesus was laying down a rule and when he was holding up an ideal. We do not always know how to marry the teaching of Jesus with more recent scientific or medical knowledge and insight. The fact is that Jesus had nothing to say about some of the ethical issues we face in the twenty-first century. To place yourself under the moral authority of the teaching of Jesus, therefore, is to commit yourself to a lifetime of exploring what he meant, of being ready to challenge conventional interpretations, while struggling to conform to teaching that seems too hard to follow. For Peter it all began with listening. It was a long time before some of what he heard turned into insightful teaching of his own. Listening, with an open mind, but with a desire to follow, is always the starting point.

Alongside the teaching, Peter encountered the power of God at work in Jesus' actions. A leper was cleansed, a centurion's servant was healed – as were two demoniacs who lived among the tombs, a paralysed man on his bed, a woman with haemorrhages, two blind men and a person who was mute. Matthew tells most of these stories succinctly, leaving out much of the detail, in order to focus on the dialogue between Jesus and the one who is being healed and to put the emphasis on what Jesus is doing: revealing himself as one who can act in the place of God. Peter witnesses over and over again this breathtaking exercise of divine power in the man he is following. It happens even in Peter's own house, when Jesus finds Peter's mother-in-law lying in bed with a fever. He touches her hand – that is all that it takes – and the fever leaves her and she begins to serve him. Word spreads fast and by evening the house is filled with those who have come for healing (Matthew 8.14–17).

Among those healing stories is one that the Gospel writers saw as having special significance for Peter. Matthew recounts it, though it is Luke who tells us that Peter was particularly close to the event. A synagogue leader, Jairus by name, comes to Jesus, begging him to come to his house to heal his dying 12-year-old daughter. Jesus consents and sets off, but before he even gets to the house, a message comes that the girl has died and that they should not trouble him further. Jesus, however, reassures them and continues to the house. Once there, he goes to the girl, taking with him only her parents and three disciples, Peter, James and John.

> They were all weeping and wailing for her; but he said, 'Do not weep; for she is not dead but sleeping.' And they laughed at him, knowing that she was dead. But he took her by the hand and called out, 'Child, get up!' Her spirit returned, and she got up at once. Then he directed them to give her something to eat.
>
> (Luke 8.52–55)

Why Peter, James and John? It's odd, when you think about it, why these three grown men – imagine them, big burly fishermen – should be crowded into the room as Jesus takes the girl by the hand and says to her, 'Child, get up.' We cannot know why they too were there, but it does almost seem that Jesus wanted the three, Peter among them, to witness a new depth to his ministry, to have the opportunity to be drawn more deeply into the mystery of his being, to see and at least to begin to believe.

And what they saw was a revelation of a Jesus who brought God's healing, who was an agent of God's salvation. They saw a wondrous miracle, the bringing back to life of a dead girl, but they saw it because it showed them the work of healing, the work of salvation, that is what God is always about, and of which Jesus was and is the agent. It gave them something wonderful, breathtaking, to talk about, to witness to. And, though perhaps at first Peter kept uncharacteristically quiet and reflected, as he was told to, in time he did talk about it – about the raising of the child, about the healing and the salvation.

Hidden among all the stories of healing that Matthew tells, there is one mighty act of power of a very different sort (8.23–27) – the stilling of a storm. Matthew, Mark and Luke all describe the incident. Jesus is asleep in the boat when a windstorm arises, a storm so powerful that the boat is being swamped. The frightened disciples wake Jesus up, desperate for him to save them. He wonders at their lack of faith, though the very fact that they believe he can save them indicates that they do have at least a little faith in him. He rebukes the winds and the sea and suddenly there is a great calm. 'What sort of man is this,' they ask, 'that even the winds and the sea obey him?' Whether it was Peter who articulated this, as it often was, or whether he reflected in silent wonder, here was another element in the formation of his understanding of Jesus and the growth of his relationship with him. A Jesus who could control the sea would turn out to be crucial for Peter and the issue of faith would soon focus on Peter alone.

So Peter has walked away from his home. He has received the teaching, he has seen the healings, he has witnessed the divine power. His life is being given a new shape. And then comes a point where Jesus' ministry – the teaching in the synagogues, the proclaiming of the kingdom of God, the curing of disease and sickness – is meeting sufficient success that Jesus, almost, it seems, overwhelmed by his own compassion and the great need of the people who are like sheep without a shepherd, says to his disciples, 'The harvest is plentiful, but the labourers are few.' He urges them to 'ask the Lord of the harvest to send out labourers into his harvest' (9.35–38). And as if in answer to the problem, he commissions 12 of these disciples to be apostles. Simon Peter is the first named among them; among the very first to be called, he is now given the priority of being the first in the list, followed by his brother Andrew, James and John. And now is the moment, because the harvest is plentiful, for the labourers to be sent out.

This is a key moment. Until now Peter and the others have simply followed. Now they are to be entrusted with a share in the ministry. Disciples themselves, they are now to disciple others. Not only is it a key moment, it is probably a moment of trepidation. They suddenly find themselves entrusted with an awesome commission, for Jesus has given them authority 'over unclean spirits, to cast them out, and to cure every disease and every sickness' (Matthew 10.1). It is a tall order, and even as he gives them this authority, Jesus recognizes that they are not yet quite ready for it. He embarks on further teaching (Matthew 10.5–42) – preparation for ministry, we might call it today – both to give them confidence and to warn them of the dangers. He is sending them out 'like sheep into the midst of wolves', so they must be 'wise as serpents and innocent as doves' (10.16). They must not be afraid, for 'even the hairs on your head are all counted' (10.30–31). But they are still disciples, and 'it is enough for the disciple to be like the teacher' (10.25).

There is an important lesson for us in the way Jesus draws people into sharing his mission. At first, if we experience a call to follow, we are allowed to do just that: follow, and not much more. We cannot on day one of our following expect to be effective co-workers (though there are some remarkable exceptions, the apostle Paul among them). Most of us need to be allowed to follow: to listen to some teaching, to assimilate it carefully, maybe question it; to see God at work – not so much perhaps in mighty acts, but in the effective ministry and the remarkable lives of those who have become God's friends; and to allow ourselves to be shaped by the Holy Spirit, little by little, into more Christ-like beings. It is a process of looking, listening, allowing ourselves to be moulded. We may at first be quite frightened even by the thought of being labelled 'disciples' – it can imply more commitment than we feel inside – but quietly we are allowing ourselves to be brought into something like the shape of Christ, beginning to acquire something of his heart and mind. That's what seemed to be happening to Peter. You can't hurry that process.

Perhaps, though, if you can't, just sometimes Jesus can. There is a bit of divine impatience sometimes that wants us to begin to share the mission quite early on in our Christian pilgrimage. Before we think ourselves ready (as if we ever would be), before we think we have questions of belief sorted out, while we are very aware that there is only a little faith, a voice within us seems to be saying, 'Come, share the work, start telling the good news.' We may not be fully formed – certainly we are not entirely conformed to Jesus Christ and his pattern – but we are invited, though it often feels like an imperative, to move from being entirely learners and recipients to being part of the mission. The reassurance lies in the fact that we are still disciples, learning on the job. Trying to be like our teacher is good enough. Becoming part of the mission is an important element in our formation. It is not an add-on; it comes, not quite on day one, but very often before we expect it.

But the time is drawing near, at least as Matthew tells it, for a moment of huge significance for Peter's relationship with Jesus. Jesus hears from the disciples of the death of John the Baptist, executed by King Herod, and responds to this news by withdrawing by boat to a deserted place. However, the crowds walk round the lake and wait for him. He has compassion on them and spends the day in curing the sick; when the evening comes he is still surrounded by the crowd, who are now in need of food. There follows the story normally known as 'the feeding of the five thousand' (Matthew 14.13–22). With just five loaves and two fish, Jesus feeds the great multitude. The occasion has something of the atmosphere of the Eucharist about it, not least in the precise way that Matthew, who so often omits the detail, describes exactly what Jesus did.

> Taking the five loaves and the two fish, he looked up to heaven, and blessed and broke the loaves, and gave them to the disciples, and the disciples gave them to the crowd. And all ate and were filled; and they took up what was left over of the broken pieces, twelve baskets full. (Matthew 14.19b–20)

Sharing food together is, of course, part of the common life you would expect of those who kept company with Jesus. Eating sufficient to live, and indeed sufficient to have the strength and energy for the mission of this itinerant community, would have been a practical necessity. But that, of course, is not the point of the story. Here we are being given, just as Peter was, yet another pointer to the divine power invested in Jesus, who can nourish and satisfy a great crowd with slender resources. We are being given, too, a picture of the kind of extended, inclusive community that the kingdom of God would bring in. This meal is for everyone – no qualifications are required, there are no limitations on who may share. All that is needed is sufficient fascination with Jesus to be there. It would take Peter a long time, and a dream that took him to the house of a Gentile called Cornelius (Acts 10), to understand just how inclusive the invitation needed to be, but the seeds of it are sown here in the feeding of the crowd on whom Jesus had compassion.

The most important lesson Peter and the disciples had to learn in that deserted place was that God's resources are sufficient to meet every human need. Jesus knew they had sufficient food to feed the crowd. But, as they found themselves drawn into this particular act of ministry, distributing the bread to the people and collecting up the broken pieces that remained, the disciples had to discover that for themselves. There was, too, the secondary lesson that the kingdom is open to everyone, that the bread of life is for all, and that the good news that Peter and the others were to proclaim is for the whole of humanity. Jesus is the companion – that is, literally, the one with whom of all people we share bread. The Church still struggles with that idea when it comes to who may share its meals.

The story sets the scene for a great drama. It is one of those rare stories told by all four Gospel writers, but only Matthew relates it to Peter. With the meal only just over and the fragments gathered up in the baskets, Jesus sends the disciples off across the lake in a boat, while he dismisses the crowd and claims some prayer time on the mountain before coming to join the disciples. He is still there on the mountainside in the evening when the wind gets up, out at sea, and the boat in which the disciples are travelling is battered by the waves. They survive this stormy night, but with the dawn comes something extraordinary.

> And early in the morning he came walking towards them on the lake. But when the disciples saw him walking on the lake, they were terrified, saying, 'It is a ghost!' And they cried out in fear. But immediately Jesus spoke to them and said, 'Take heart, it is I; do not be afraid.'
>
> Peter answered him, 'Lord, if it is you, command me to come to you on the water.' He said, 'Come.' So Peter got out of the boat, started walking on the water, and came towards Jesus. But when he noticed the strong wind, he became frightened, and beginning to sink, he cried out, 'Lord, save me!' Jesus immediately reached out his hand and caught him, saying to him, 'You of little faith, why did you doubt?' When they got into the boat, the wind ceased. And those in the boat worshipped him, saying, 'Truly you are the Son of God.' (Matthew 14.25–33)

At first this feels like a great reversal for Peter. All through the previous chapters he has been listening to the teaching of Jesus, witnessing great events and being drawn deeper into relationship and into mission, and now comes a great failure. Perhaps so, but there are some very positive things here too.

First, there is Peter's desire to identify with Jesus, to be a disciple who imitates the teacher. Jesus walks on the water, so Peter wants to do the same. To follow the teacher is what a disciple tries to do. Second, Peter wants to act in a way that meets with Jesus' approval. So he does not simply climb out of the boat on his own initiative. His desire is there, but he waits for Jesus' command. Only when Jesus indicates what he wants Peter to do does Peter respond to the imperative, 'Come!' These are signs that Peter is learning what it means to be a disciple.

So, responding to Jesus, he launches out into the deep. For a moment he walks confidently on the water, in a way very different from that Easter occasion when at breakfast time he will climb out of the boat and wade with heavy steps through the water to Jesus, who is waiting on the shore (John 21.7). But his confidence lasts only a moment; soon the strong wind frightens him and he begins to sink. And later Jesus will upbraid him for the littleness of his faith: 'You of little faith' – Jesus has used the phrase of his disciples before and he will use it again, but here it is addressed to Peter alone. Yet we need to regard even these words in a positive light. Peter does demonstrate a little faith – sufficient to climb out of the boat, sufficient to take an enormous risk, though not enough to finish what he started.

I believe God honours our little faith. We may, like the father with the sick child whom Jesus met in Mark 9.24, find ourselves saying, 'I believe, help my unbelief', but God honours the faith we have and wants us to use it, wants to enable it to make us courageous and take risks – risks in terms of faith, commitment and life-changing decisions. Little faith can grow into large faith.

It is more likely to do so if we take risks with it. Part of such faith is, of course, that if – when – it falters, collapses even, there is a God who will come to our rescue and pick us up.

In that moment of panic, when the little faith was not enough, Peter could do nothing but cry out to Jesus to save him. Yet even that revealed some faith; though he spoke out of his terror, he spoke also in response to a Jesus who had already urged the disciples not to be afraid. 'Take heart, it is I; do not be afraid,' Jesus had said. 'It is I' is the same use of the 'I am who I am' name for God that Jesus adopts elsewhere, especially in the Fourth Gospel. This is the Son of God who is coming to the rescue. Jesus stretches out his hand and draws Peter back into the boat. Peter has demonstrated his faith, insufficient as it is, but now has experienced the divine rescue of a drowning man.

It was another lesson for the disciple, at least for the disciple of this particular master, for this master was revealing himself to be more than a teacher, certainly more than an exemplar. Those in the boat, Matthew tells us, responded to what they had seen – Jesus walking on the water, Jesus saving Peter, Jesus causing the wind to cease – by one of those amazing affirmations, the significance of which is easy to miss if you move on too quickly. The affirmation came in what they did and what they said. For what they did was to 'worship' or to 'pay homage'. It is the first time the disciples are recorded as doing such a thing. Magi from the east did it at Bethlehem many years before when following the star to a new-born king (Matthew 2.11); a man with leprosy had done it, finding himself healed (8.2); the synagogue leader with the epileptic son had done it (9.18). But now the disciples do it for the first time – they pay homage, they worship. They will do it again, of course, when Jesus takes his leave of them after the resurrection (28.17), but it is this sequence of events on the water that first brings out this collective response among them. They express it, too, in words: 'Truly you are the Son of God!' It is the first time they have said those words.

Despite the focus on Peter in the story, Matthew does not say that Peter said it. Perhaps we are to picture Peter, wet and bedraggled, sensing his failure, crawling into the corner of the boat, not ready yet to say anything at all. But it will not be long before he has the chance to make that same affirmation alone, and probably he will need to do so.

There is much here to reflect on for anyone moving into faith and commitment. Have I sufficient faith to launch out into the deep? Is my trust in God sufficient to take risks, knowing that there is one who can rescue and save me? Have I the self-knowledge and the humility to allow Jesus to be my saviour, or must I still try to save myself alone? And have I reached the point when I can give Jesus homage and worship and call him 'Son of God'?

If the answer to these questions is yes, even a quiet tentative yes that comes out of a little faith, this could be the moment to move into an exploration of belonging. It may even be the moment to think seriously about baptism, which, among other things, draws a person formally into the Christian community. The Gospels do not describe the disciples being baptized, though it does describe them baptizing others (John 4.2), and baptism as entry to the Church is well established from the day of Pentecost (Acts 2.38). But what happens to Peter here in the water has a baptismal quality about it. Though people often associate baptism with cleansing, the fundamental image of Christian baptism, in Scripture and in the life of the Church, is one of drowning; or, more precisely, of being rescued from the drowning waters by the saving Christ. There is a moment when, recognizing our need, we want Jesus to stretch out his hand to draw us into the boat and we know we have sufficient faith to ask for that. That is the moment for us to seek baptism – or, if we were baptized long ago, to seek to reaffirm our baptism, perhaps professing our faith afresh, perhaps being sprinkled with water from the font, perhaps by anointing. It is another step on the path to becoming God's friend.

Of course it may not yet be the moment when yes is the answer to those questions. But for Peter, with his little faith, rescued from the water by one whom the disciples called Son of God, the time is ripe for another conversion.

3

Take up your cross and follow

It has been a moment of huge significance. Peter has tried to walk on the water and, when his faith has failed, Jesus has rescued him. The disciples in the boat, witnessing the whole sequence of events, worship Jesus and acknowledge that he is the Son of God. Everything will now be different, better perhaps.

But it is not going to be so, and the next phase of Peter's following of Jesus has some things to teach us about how hard discipleship can be. There is a lesson about how, just when we have made a leap forward, somehow we seem to find ourselves back where we were. There's an insight about how, often, we don't dig deep enough for truth and so get it all wrong and fail to understand. There's a crucial and sobering message about the fact that the call to 'Follow me' is often preceded by the rather scary command 'Take up your cross', with its hint that there is suffering in store for the disciple as well as for the master. And there's a call to something involving discipline – prayer, without which the disciple cannot move forward.

So, with Peter's rescue from the water behind him, will his discipleship move into a different phase? Unfortunately no. That moment of crisis for Peter and of illumination for the other disciples is quickly followed by a return to the ordinary round of healing and teaching, as if nothing much has changed. Sick people receive healing from Jesus just by touching the fringes of his cloak. Jesus continues to teach, now more often by engaging in dispute – Pharisees and scribes are challenging him and demanding a sign. It's very much business as usual, though now with a hint that a storm is brewing.

Jesus tells the crowd, 'It is not what goes into the mouth that defiles a person, but what comes out of the mouth that defiles.' The Pharisees are offended and the disciples are puzzled. It's Peter who articulates their need for elucidation. 'Explain this parable to us,' he says to Jesus, and in response Jesus replies, 'Are you still without understanding?' A Canaanite woman comes to Jesus and, despite the message of inclusion contained in the feeding of the multitude, Jesus at first holds back from welcoming her in order to test her. The disciples want to send her away, though when she does reach Jesus, she turns out to be a woman of insight and faith. Yet nothing seems to have changed. Whatever is going on inside, on the outside Peter is still getting it wrong. The disciples are still failing to get the message. The epiphany experience of walking on the water is quite forgotten and we are back in a world of dispute, misunderstanding and very little faith. It will need another miracle feeding in the desert to turn that round again.

What we are seeing here is something common to Christian discipleship. We experience extraordinary moments when there is a jump forward in faith, a shaft of insight, a powerful sense of rescue – a deep experience, maybe, of the reality of God. But instead of leading us into life lived on a higher plane, such moments are followed by a return to the ordinary and the humdrum. The extraordinary moment seems to evaporate. We may be deeply disappointed in ourselves and, if the truth be told, deeply disappointed in God. But you cannot live always on the mountain top. Peter is to learn that, literally, all too soon. The moments of grace help to make sense of the unspectacular, day-to-day times and places, when we don't seem to make much progress on our spiritual journey. But the unspectacular, day-to-day times and places are where we need to live most of our lives. They are the times and places where we can be faithful and do most good.

But now there follows another of those extraordinary moments. It feels as if it follows on from the walking on the water, for it picks up on the disciples' affirmation of Jesus as the Son of God, though disputes and misunderstandings, as well as healings, have intervened. This time it is all about Peter. It is his chance to make his profession of faith. It happens at Caesarea Philippi, on the southern slope of Mount Hermon at one of the sources of the River Jordan – a city previously named Panion, with a shrine to the god Pan, but now to be recognized in the Christian world as a place of divine revelation of the true God and his anointed Son. Jesus asks his disciples who people think he is. He is given a variety of answers – John the Baptist, Elijah, Jeremiah or another of the prophets. Then he asks a different question. Not 'Who do people say I am?', but 'Who do you say I am?' He asks it of them all, but it is Peter who replies, 'You are the Messiah, the Son of the living God.'

From Jesus it produces this affirming response:

> Blessed are you, Simon son of Jonah! For flesh and blood has not revealed this to you, but my Father in heaven. And I tell you, you are Peter, and on this rock I will build my church, and the gates of Hades will not prevail against it. I will give you the keys of the kingdom of heaven, and whatever you bind on earth will be bound in heaven, and whatever you loose on earth will be loosed in heaven. (Matthew 16.17–19)

But with it comes an order not to tell anyone.

Mark and Luke record this incident too, but Matthew makes more of it, not least in the 'beatitude' of Peter – 'Blessed are you, Simon, son of Jonah.' Although Jesus has called all those who follow him 'blessed' in the beatitudes that open the Sermon on the Mount (5.1–12), this is the one and only occasion when an individual is described in this way and it gives Peter a special place among the apostles. It is all the more surprising, given that Peter has so recently been upbraided for his little faith and his failure to understand. But it is done in response to the declaration about who Jesus is. Peter calls him 'Messiah' (or 'the Christ') and 'Son of the living God'. Although Matthew has already used the term 'messiah' for Jesus, this is the first time that one of the disciples so describes him.

Both *masiah* in Hebrew and *Christos* in Greek mean 'the anointed one'. It had a number of different meanings in Jesus' day; there was no one clear understanding. But one prominent belief was of a future king, in the line of David, who would restore justice and the good fortunes of God's people. Such a messiah would, of course, be a threat both to the Roman occupying forces and to the Jewish collaborating establishment. This was the kind of messiah many longed for and the evangelists imply that people were beginning to see Jesus in this light. Whether Peter means exactly this, or whether we should see his emphasis as being on Jesus' relationship with the Father, the anointed one of God, we cannot know, but certainly both Peter himself and then Jesus provide a gloss on the meaning of 'messiah' as far as it relates to Jesus.

Peter's own gloss comes when he adds the words 'the Son of the living God'. The amazing truth is that this is the anointed Son of God. The disciples have said it already when Jesus walked on the water. They have worshipped him and found themselves saying, 'You are the Son of God.' And now Peter has his chance to say it, all on his own, to say it straight. It is a kind of rehearsal for the encounter at breakfast on the beach. There Peter, having deserted and denied his master, will respond to Jesus' questioning with a declaration of friendship. Here Peter, having failed his master when his faith deserted him, responds to Jesus' questioning with a declaration of faith. The point is not so much that he says what has not been said before, though it is the first time Jesus has been called 'Messiah', but more that it is Peter who has said it, Peter who has been restored.

Just as on the lakeside, Jesus responds with affirmation. This is the moment, for Matthew, when Simon becomes Peter, the Rock, a rock on which the Christian community will be built. It is a prophecy that will have ample fulfilment in the post-resurrection Church. This Church will not be overcome by the 'gates of Hades', that is, by death or the powers opposed to God. Peter is given here, as the whole body of disciples is given a little later (18.18), the power to 'bind and loose', whether to make rules and grant exceptions or, as in the Fourth Gospel (John 20.23), to withhold forgiveness. The intention is to say that God will ratify and stand behind what Peter, and later the others, decide.

Gradually, from his first call, through the period of formation of his discipleship, Peter has been learning what it means to follow Christ. He has also been learning – and it has been a hard lesson – about his own weakness and his dependence on Jesus, who rescues him and restores him. More profoundly still, he has been discovering who this Jesus is. He is more than rabbi, more than master. He is the Christ, the Son of the living God. It is a wonderful profession of faith. Peter has arrived where he needs to be. It is a turning point, not just for Peter, but for the whole company of disciples. For no sooner has Jesus accepted the title of Messiah (though they are to tell no one) than he introduces a new message that changes the whole direction of his life and transforms what it means for them to be his followers:

> From that time on, Jesus began to show his disciples that he must go to Jerusalem and undergo great suffering at the hands of the elders and chief priests and scribes, and be killed, and on the third day be raised. (Matthew 16.21)

In Luke the disciples accept what he says and Jesus goes on to build on this teaching (Luke 9.21–22). But in Matthew (and in Mark) Peter intervenes:

> And Peter took [Jesus] aside and began to rebuke him, saying, 'God forbid it, Lord! This must never happen to you.' But he turned and said to Peter, 'Get behind me, Satan! You are a stumbling-block to me; for you are setting your mind not on divine things but on human things.' (Matthew 16.22–23)

If Peter has put a gloss on the meaning of messiahship with his addition of 'the Son of the living God', Jesus now adds his own much more radical reshaping of the concept. For there was at that time no association of the messiah with suffering. It is a later Christian understanding that brought together the role of messiah with the suffering servant portrayed by Isaiah. Peter, not unnaturally, fails to cope with this twist immediately and so, having one moment been a rock, becomes immediately a stumbling-block. It's hard on Peter. He has just affirmed that Jesus is a divine being, the Son of God, yet a moment later he is being told that his mind is not on the divine. He has not yet discerned the mind of God. Matthew doesn't call Jesus' response a rebuke in the way that Mark does, but Jesus hears in Peter's protest the same inner temptation he is himself experiencing to turn aside from the path of suffering, and expresses it in the language he has used when tempted in the wilderness – 'Away with you, get behind me, Satan!' (Matthew 4.10; 16.23).

Peter is the first to be told very firmly that he has got it wrong and that there is a new and challenging truth to be assimilated. Perhaps this is because Peter's path of suffering is going to be particularly acute, both in following – or failing to follow – Jesus to Jesus' cross, and also later in following a similar path to his own cross. But it is not only Peter who needs to begin to understand this new truth that Jesus is introducing. All the disciples need to hear it and ponder over it. They have to learn, Peter has to learn, that the attractive call to 'follow me' has now taken on a more sober tone. Now it is 'take up your cross and follow me'.

> Jesus told his disciples, 'If any want to become my followers, let them deny themselves and take up their cross and follow me. For those who want to save their life will lose it, and those who lose their life for my sake will find it. For what will it profit them if they gain the whole world but forfeit their life? Or what will they give in return for their life?'   (Matthew 16.24–26)

There is a change of tempo in the Gospel now and a change of direction; or, more exactly, there is now, for the first time, a very clear sense of direction. The itinerant ministry is over. Jesus has told the disciples that he must go to Jerusalem, and that now becomes the geographical objective. There is a spiritual objective too, spelt out with equal clarity, to undergo great suffering and be killed, and to be raised on the third day. It will take time for them to assimilate this. Jesus will not tell them just once. 'From that time on' (16.21) he will help them understand that this has to be the case. Three times Jesus gives what have come to be called 'the predictions of the Passion'. In each case the disciples fail to comprehend. On this first occasion it is Peter who expresses dismay. Later Jesus will foretell his death again, at which the disciples are 'greatly distressed' (17.22–23). The third time, which is even more precise and speaks of Jesus being handed over to the Gentiles 'to be mocked and flogged and crucified', their misunderstanding is so basic that they turn the subject round to one about sitting on Jesus' right and left in the kingdom.

Peter has gained a deeper understanding of who Jesus is, accompanied by the grace to confess it openly. Alongside that

there has been a corrective from Jesus, and building on that
corrective, a new agenda – for the Anointed One is to suffer. This
is another of those key moments, a change of gear. It is expressed
succinctly in the new version of the call, 'Take up your cross
and follow me.' For Peter this means entering the new territory
of a Jesus who suffers and invites his followers to suffer with
him, a Jesus who will be sacrificed and invites sacrifices of
his disciples.

That is where we too can find ourselves in our journey to
embrace faith and commit to Jesus Christ. For some that
element of the call is present from the beginning. The road
looks like a road to Calvary from the very start and it requires
immense courage to begin to walk it. But for most of us
the road begins as an appealing one, following the attractive
teacher and healer – a Jesus utterly alive, filled with the Spirit,
a Jesus who brings joy and delight and shows us the Father.
Following him is not so difficult; it can be liberating and
fulfilling as nothing else can.

But then we hear his words about suffering and see him
walking resolutely towards a cross and, on the way to it, experiencing loneliness, pain, humiliation and something approaching
despair. The going suddenly seems very tough and the temptation
to walk away is strong, especially if, unlike the Jesus portrayed
by the evangelists, we can't see the light at the end of the
tunnel. The empty tomb is veiled from sight; only the cross
looks real. Of course, many scholars reckon that the talk of
resurrection on the third day in these predictions of the Passion
was added by the Church after Jesus had risen from the dead.
Did he go to his death with a clear view of what would happen
on the third day? Perhaps not, though he would have known
that the path he was treading would lead almost inevitably
to his death and would have moved towards it with trust in

a faithful God. That's what we are sometimes called to do. It is the cost of discipleship.

Maybe Peter was beginning to grasp that fact, for this time we do not hear him leading the protests as Jesus foretells the Passion. What may have helped him is the next epiphany, another moment of revelation given to that same trio – Peter and James and John – who had witnessed Jesus raise a young girl from death. It comes only six days after that first occasion when Jesus shared with them the destiny that awaited him in Jerusalem. It is the event we call the Transfiguration. The four of them go up the mountain (probably Mount Hermon, though traditionally Mount Tabor) and suddenly they see Jesus in an entirely new way, as if through a heavenly lens. His face shines, his clothing becomes dazzling white. There is, for the evangelists, no other word for it than 'transfiguration'. With equal suddenness Jesus is no longer ahead of them alone, but with him are two great figures of the Old Covenant, Moses and Elijah. It is Peter, inevitably, who speaks:

> 'Lord, it is good for us to be here; if you wish, I will make three dwellings here, one for you, one for Moses, and one for Elijah.' While he was still speaking, suddenly a bright cloud overshadowed them, and from the cloud a voice said, 'This is my Son, the Beloved; with him I am well pleased; listen to him!' When the disciples heard this, they fell to the ground and were overcome by fear. But Jesus came and touched them, saying, 'Get up and do not be afraid.' And when they looked up, they saw no one except Jesus himself alone.   (Matthew 17.4–8)

The 'six days' point us back to Exodus, where the glory of the Lord in a cloud covered Mount Sinai for six days (24.16), when Moses was with God on the mountain, his face shining as the face of Jesus did at the Transfiguration, and where God spoke to him as a friend. In Exodus 33.11, one of those little verses

34

of Scripture you might easily miss, we are told that 'the Lord used to speak to Moses face to face, as one speaks to a friend.' And here, on this mountain, God is revealing the glory Jesus shares with him and speaking face to face with Peter, James and John. It is, perhaps, an invitation into friendship.

This is another experience of the glory of God, this time in the face of Jesus Christ. It is an extraordinarily rich story, in which every line, and every variation in the three Gospel accounts of it, is full of symbolism and meaning. But we need here to focus principally on the role of Peter and what it meant for him.

So let us look at what Peter says and how the disciples respond to the 'vision', as Jesus himself calls it (Matthew 17.9). Peter exclaims, 'Lord, it is good for us to be here.' We need go no further than the first word to find something significant. Peter addresses Jesus as 'Lord'. Peter is drawing on his understanding, proclaimed at Caesarea Philippi, that Jesus is a divine being. Of course, the use of such an address increases the gap between Peter and Jesus. If Jesus is master and lord, what does that make Peter? It is a question they will soon have to address. Some commentators see in Peter's 'It is good for us to be here' another example of his need to say something, whether appropriate or not, where others might choose to remain silent, recognizing that any words would be inadequate. But surely Peter is getting it absolutely right. This is a huge privilege for Peter, James and John, for they are being invited into a moment that transcends time and space. It is a preview of a glory that will belong to Jesus at the end of time, when God's kingdom is realized in all its fullness. It is indeed a heavenly vision. 'It is good for us to be here' is a beautiful understatement.

There follows another of those instances where Peter wants Jesus to direct his actions. Just as he needed Jesus to tell him to come when he walked on the water, now he needs Jesus to say whether it might be appropriate to build the three dwellings – pitch the three tents. He will do it only 'if you wish'. Both Mark and Luke are clear that Peter is searching for the right words, telling us that he did not know what to say (Mark 9.6; Luke 9.33); and, of course, they are right. Nevertheless Matthew wisely omits their comment, for there is a lovely intimacy here: the three disciples caught up in a heavenly vision, finding it wonderful and amazing to be there, seeing Jesus in glory and wanting to say and do the right thing. There is a gentleness too, and a hint of Easter, in the way Jesus responds to the way they have been overwhelmed: 'Jesus came and touched them.' Only here and at his appearance as the risen Lord (28.18) do we read in Matthew that Jesus 'comes to' the disciples. He comes, so to speak, as Lord over death and raises them up. It is what will happen again to Peter when, at Easter, Jesus needs to raise him up after the death-like denial of the night before his crucifixion. Here, to strengthen the disciples for what lies ahead, is a prefiguring of the resurrection.

What can all this have meant to Peter, either there and then or later as he reflected on it? He is still reflecting on it, if they are his authentic words, in the Second Letter of Peter years later, where we read:

> We did not follow cleverly devised myths when we made known to you the power and coming of our Lord Jesus Christ, but we had been eyewitnesses of his majesty. For he received honour and glory from God the Father when that voice was conveyed to him by the Majestic Glory, saying, 'This is my Son, my Beloved, with whom I am well pleased.' We ourselves heard this voice come from heaven, while we were with him on the holy mountain. (2 Peter 1.16–18)

First Peter receives divine confirmation of his own confession that Jesus is God's Son. Peter proclaimed it. Now he hears the voice of God say the very same thing – 'This is my Son, the

Beloved.' It is the same declaration as Jesus heard at his baptism, at the beginning of his itinerant ministry. He hears it again now, as his mission takes on a different shape. Peter hears it too, but with the additional imperative, 'Listen to him.' Peter must hear what Jesus is saying, and Peter knows what that is, because it is the very last thing he heard before they climbed the mountain. It was the message about the suffering and death of Jesus and about the need for those who would be his disciples to take up the cross and follow. The divinity was confirmed, but so was the suffering. Peter had to listen to that. As they come down from the mountain and fall into conversation with Jesus, it becomes clear that the presence of Elijah, alongside Moses, in the vision has been related to the suffering that awaits Jesus. 'I tell you that Elijah has already come, and they did not recognize him, but they did to him whatever they pleased,' he says. And he adds, 'so also the Son of Man is about to suffer at their hands' (17.12). Yes, Peter has to accept that what Jesus has said about suffering and the cross is going to happen.

Yet he is also given a glimpse of glory, a brief and daring anticipation of the risen, ascended and glorified Lord. Whether he could make sense of such an epiphany at that moment, we can only speculate, but later he certainly understood it. He knew he had been an eyewitness of Christ's majesty.

Not everyone is privileged – as part of their journey into faith, or later, along the path of discipleship – to have what you might call a 'transfiguration experience'. But it does happen, often unexpectedly, that there is a moment when our sense of God and God's glory become intensely real, almost visible and physical, even if only fleetingly. Mountain tops, or at least the open air, are often the setting for such moments, though they may come also inside a church or during the offering of worship. Sometimes they come, with all their beauty, into a situation that seems quite ugly – but that situation is trans-figured. Such a moment may give a sense of the friendship of God – 'talking face to face as with a friend' in the way Moses experienced it. But such moments are not for everybody. Even among the apostles, only three were granted that revelation, and they were not to speak about it. So we should not be anxious if there has been no shaft of light for us. In any case, the message of the transfiguration story is that a revelation is momentary and is always followed by a return to the humdrum of daily living. Jesus, Peter and the others came down the moun-tain straight into human need and a situation that was anything but glorious, that demanded prayer and fasting – a child in need of healing.

Now is the moment where – for all the danger of moving from one Gospel writer to another without remembering they have different theological intentions – it is time to take leave of Matthew, who has given us compelling pictures of Peter as Jesus walks on the water, receives Peter's confession of faith at Caesarea Philippi and is transfigured on the mountain, and to spend a few moments with Luke before moving to the Fourth Gospel as the Passion approaches.

We must move to Luke in order to ensure we do not miss something crucial about prayer. For at several important points in Peter's discipleship, Luke puts an emphasis on Jesus at prayer. In Luke 6.12, where he is about to choose his 12 apostles, 'Simon whom he named Peter' first among them, Jesus 'went out to the mountain to pray; and he spent the night in prayer to God'. In Luke 9.18, it is the prayer that causes Jesus to ask his disciples who the crowds believe he is: 'Once when Jesus was praying alone, with only the disciples near him, he asked them, "Who do the crowds say that I am?"' Later, in Luke 11.1, we find Jesus 'praying in a certain place, and after he had finished, one of his disciples said to him, "Lord, teach us to pray".' Later still, of course, in Gethsemane on the night of his arrest, Jesus invites the disciples to pray and then withdraws from them about a stone's throw, kneeling down and praying (Luke 22.41). Between those first two and last two instances of Jesus at prayer comes the Transfiguration. As Luke sees it, the whole event is a prayer experience. Jesus went up the mountain to pray and it was while he was praying that his appearance changed and his clothes became dazzling white (Luke 9.28–29). Part of what Peter witnessed over and over again was Jesus at prayer. Part of what he knew shaped and resourced Jesus was his intimate prayer with the Father. No wonder the disciples wanted to pray and listened eagerly as Jesus taught them to pray. Prayer is a necessary part of discipleship.

The ability to pray does not come automatically with the call to follow Jesus. For some it seems to be the most natural thing in the world. That must be a huge blessing. For most of us, however, even beginning to pray is a challenge and we must not become disheartened by imagining that every other would-be follower of Jesus has a well-developed, satisfying prayer life. Most of us are still not far down the path of prayer. Many of us know ourselves to be novices. Some of us have given up the practice of prayer at times, or else, when nothing more personal and spontaneous seems to rise up within us, have been carried along only by the Church's liturgical prayer. Though the Gospel writers, especially Luke and John, portray a Jesus for whom prayer is the lifeline to the Father, they do not describe the company who followed Jesus as a praying community. Perhaps when Jesus was with them they were carried by his prayer. But by the time of the Acts of the Apostles, prayer has become central and crucial to the life of the Christian community, as we shall see. For those of us who do not have the historical Jesus as our focus, walking in our company, the need to reach up to the Father with him and through him is vital. We may be only apprentices when it comes to prayer, but – as Luke can teach us – we must get started and then persevere. Without it we may be disciples stuck at the starting blocks.

One other very important verse from Luke's Gospel can take us from the Transfiguration to what lies ahead for Jesus and for Peter. It comes after the second of those predictions of the Passion, after Jesus, Peter, James and John have come down from the mountain. 'When the days drew near for him to be taken up, he set his face to go to Jerusalem,' Luke tells us (9.51). It sums up the transition that has come about through the events at Caesarea Philippi and on the mountain. The King James Bible adds the word 'steadfastly' to the translation. He has set his face steadfastly towards Jerusalem. Peter is going with him.

4

Servants no longer

I want now to shift the ground considerably and to look at Peter's relationship with Jesus from a very different angle – not least because, as the Fourth Gospel portrays it, I believe the relationship does, through the days of Jesus' Passion, change and deepen very significantly. It will mean a move from the writers of the synoptic Gospels, from Matthew, Mark and Luke, to the very different Fourth Gospel that bears the name of John. It will also mean a move from talk of discipleship to talk of friendship – not that the Fourth Gospel is neglectful of discipleship, but it does move us towards a point where Jesus calls his disciples not servants, but friends.

Deep human friendship is a wonderful gift, one that enriches our lives. It is a relationship in which there is trust, affection, mutuality, permission to be vulnerable, permission sometimes to be unreasonable and yet still be loved. A relationship that will sometimes be marked by stimulating conversation, sometimes by shared silence, sometimes by an embrace, most often by simply being at ease.

Before plunging into John's Gospel and the words of Jesus, I want to share what that wise English saint Aelred had to say about human friendship. Aelred was a twelfth-century monk, abbot of the beautiful abbey of Rievaulx, now in ruins in Yorkshire. This is what Aelred wrote in *The Mirror of Charity*:

It is such a great joy to have the consolation of someone's affection, someone to whom one is deeply united by the bonds of love; someone in whom our weary spirit may find rest, and to whom we may pour out our soul, someone whose conversation is as sweet as a song in the tedium of daily life. Such a friend will be a refuge to creep into when the world is too much for us; someone to whom we can confide all our thoughts. Their presence is a gift, a comforting kiss that heals the sickness of our preoccupied hearts. A friend will always be on hand to consult in times of uncertainty.

In fact we are so deeply bound to our friends in our hearts that even when they are far away, we feel united in spirit, together and yet alone. The world may fall asleep all around you, but you will experience your soul at rest, embraced by a profound peace. Your two hearts will lie quiet together, united as if they were one, as the grace of the Holy Spirit flows over you both.

(*The Mirror of Charity*, III, 35)

Jesus offers us something like that when he says, 'You are my friends.' God looks for something like that when he yearns for us to become God's friend. In John 15, in the very heart of what we have come to call Jesus' Farewell Discourses, when he has spoken of himself as the true vine, his Father as the vine-grower and his hearers as the branches, he brings together three significant words, disciple, servant and friend – all of them enveloped by love. This is how he joins them:

My Father is glorified by this, that you bear much fruit and become my disciples. As the Father has loved me, so I have loved you; abide in my love. If you keep my commandments, you will abide in my love, just as I have kept my Father's commandments and abide in his love. I have said these things to you so that my joy may be in you, and that your joy may be complete. This is my commandment, that you love one another as I have loved you. No one has greater love than this, to lay down one's life for one's friends. You are my friends if you do what I command you. I do not call you servants any longer, because the servant does not know what the master is doing; but I have called you friends, because I have made known to you everything that I have heard from my Father.   (John 15.8–15)

We need to remind ourselves of Peter as the writer of the Fourth Gospel perceives him. Peter is mentioned by John in only six chapters. John, for instance, doesn't tell the story of the Transfiguration and Peter's part in it, nor does he have any version of the great affirmation of faith in Jesus as the Christ at Caesarea Philippi. No, for John this is Peter:

In John 1, as we noted earlier, Peter is called into discipleship. It doesn't happen quite as the other evangelists tell it, for here Peter is brought to Jesus by his brother. There is no further mention of Peter until John 6, where there is a passing reference to 'Andrew, Simon Peter's brother', because it is Andrew who, in the Fourth Gospel, brings to Jesus the lad with the loaves and the fish that will feed the five thousand. But then, at the end of the chapter, comes the following exchange. The background is that Jesus is teaching about eating his flesh and drinking his blood, which has offended some of his hearers; some of them, even some of the disciples, have gone away, unable to cope with the teaching. Jesus finds himself asking whether the remaining disciples will go too. Peter asks a counter question and makes a great affirmation of his faith. 'Lord, to whom can we go?' he says. 'You have the words of eternal life. We have come to believe and know that you are the Holy One of God' (John 6.66).

For me that is almost Caesarea Philippi: the 'Holy One of God', rather than 'the Son of the living God'. It is all we hear of Peter until he becomes a central figure as the drama of Holy Week and Easter unfolds. In John 18 there will be his denial. In John 19 there is no mention of him because he does not make it to the foot of the cross; only the women and the Beloved Disciple stand their ground there. In John 20 he and that same disciple somewhat competitively discover the empty tomb. And then in John 21 there is the all-important encounter by the lakeside. But before that, in John 13, comes the first mention of Peter after his affirmation of faith and commitment, 'You have the words of eternal life, you are the Holy One of God.'

It is Passover time. Jesus knows that his life and ministry are building to their climax. Judas is going to betray him. The cross lies before him, and beyond it the return to the Father. He is with his disciples in the upstairs room, sharing supper. During the meal, Jesus leaves his place at the table, removes his outer garment, ties a towel around himself, pours water into a basin and one by one comes to his disciples, washes their feet and dries them with the towel. One by one till he comes to Peter.

> He came to Simon Peter, who said to him, 'Lord, are you going to wash my feet?' Jesus answered, 'You do not know now what I am doing, but later you will understand.' Peter said to him, 'You will never wash my feet.' Jesus answered, 'Unless I wash you, you have no share with me.' Simon Peter said to him, 'Lord, not my feet only but also my hands and my head!' Jesus said to him, 'One who has bathed does not need to wash, except for the feet, but is entirely clean. And you are clean, though not all of you.' For he knew who was going to betray him; for this reason he said, 'Not all of you are clean.' (John 13.6–11)

When he has completed the task, he puts on the outer garment again, returns to his place, looks at the disciples – who are moved, though perhaps also puzzled, by what he has done – and spells out his message. They call him 'Teacher' and 'Lord', and that is exactly what he is. What he is teaching them today is that they should follow his example: they should wash one another's feet, just as he has washed theirs.

The washing of feet in the communities of Jesus' day was the task of slaves. Because of that, when we reflect on this story we sometimes speak of it as an act of service. It may lead us, indeed, to talk about Jesus modelling servant leadership; I've often used it that way myself. But it has never seemed to me that service is quite what Jesus is modelling here as he kneels among his disciples.

Sometimes (and this is getting nearer the truth), we see it as modelling humility. After all, this master on his knees is the lord of heaven and earth. This is God incarnate who is washing their feet. I have always liked that reversal of roles from Bethlehem to Jerusalem. In Bethlehem at Christmas the working men, the shepherds, get down on their knees to the new-born Christ. In Jerusalem at Easter it is the Christ, as he moves towards his Passion, who gets down on his knees to the working men, the tax collector and the fishermen. So, yes, there is some modelling of humility here. But still it does not get quite to the heart of what he is doing.

The heart of it is that what he models is love, because he has taken the task away from the slave, not in order to be the slave, but to show that this is a task for a friend. Jesus does this because of friendship. Then he helps the disciples, the ones who are no longer servants but friends, to see its meaning. He talks at length with them in the Farewell Discourse in the following chapters of John, where he calls them friends and helps them to see that their relationship is not about servitude, but about friendship.

Crucial to our understanding of this passage is how we understand the Greek word *diakonia*, usually translated as 'servant'. It is important to understand that in a Christian context *diakonia* cannot involve the services of a slave or hired hand. The act is always performed by a family member, a social equal or a friend. Illustrative of this is the marriage feast at Cana, another of John's stories (John 2.1–11). The *diakonoi* who are in charge of the wine are not servants or slaves. They are the bridegroom's best friends, performing a similar service as groomsmen and bridesmaids do in weddings today, where no one is under the illusion that they are servants or slaves. So here in the washing of feet, Jesus is saying, in effect, that this kind of ministering is not a task for a slave, but for a friend. He is saying to those whose feet he washes, 'I am your friend.' It is an act of love.

There is more than one theory to account for Peter's reluctance to allow Jesus to wash his feet. Is it because he has not understood and thinks Jesus is inappropriately playing the slave? Or is it that he understands only too well that this is Jesus offering friendship with all its openness, its vulnerability and its affection, and he is not sure he is ready for such a relationship? Perhaps there is too much intimacy in the air. Jesus will not, however, let him go. Peter has to understand that what is at stake is 'having a share' with Jesus. It is almost certainly a reference to the baptismal relationship, which begins in water and involves having a part in the self-giving love that will bring Jesus to the cross. And when Peter begins to understand what Jesus is saying, or at least to understand that this foot-washing is necessary even if he does not grasp its significance, he wants to be fully involved. He grasps at the grace on offer – 'Lord, not my feet only but also my hands and my head.' Wash all of me!

Jesus has not, at this point, abandoned the roles of Teacher, Master or Lord. Indeed he specifically reminds them that that is what he is. Nor is he inviting them to think of themselves as no longer disciples. In fact, in instructing them to do what he has done and to wash one another's feet, he is asking them to be disciples in following his example. He may not call them servants, but he is not asking them to lose the capacity to serve. After all, they are to follow him, while he himself has come 'not to be served, but to serve, and to give his life as a ransom for many' (Matthew 20.28). But he is now inviting them into a relationship deeper than any of these: to be his friends and to accept his friendship, a relationship of a much more intimate and vulnerable kind, one that will transform the way they understand his role as teacher, servant and lord and their own roles as servants and disciples. Jesus is introducing a new understanding of servanthood and friendship as synonymous, with boundaries that blur into a new understanding of discipleship and lordship.

What Jesus says to Peter is, of course, what he says to any who are trying to be his followers. As soon as they can cope with such a thought, even if it challenges them, he says, in effect, 'I am your friend. I offer you the intimacy of friendship. Become, or become more deeply, God's friend.' Jesus wants each one of us to know he is our friend. He offers us the intimacy of friendship and he gives us a way into friendship with his Father, for he yearns for each one of us to be intimately God's friend. Peter is stunned by this revelation, as perhaps are we.

After the washing of the disciples' feet, this act of friendship, comes the supper. Luke tells us that it was Peter and John whom Jesus sent to prepare the meal. They were directed to a large furnished upstairs room in a house in the city and made the preparations as Jesus directed them. There Jesus institutes the Lord's Supper, speaking of the bread as his body and the cup of wine as his blood. Matthew, Mark and Luke tell the story; John simply implies it. It is within the context of the meal that Simon Peter tries to discover who it is who will betray Jesus. He signals to the disciple reclining next to Jesus to ask Jesus who he means. Jesus says that 'it is the one to whom I give this piece of bread when I have dipped it in the dish' (John 13.26).

Jesus, as the Church of England's Eucharistic Prayers put it, 'came to table with his friends' (*Common Worship*, Order 1, Prayers D and G) or 'had supper with his friends' (Prayer E). He has washed their feet. He is beginning to talk about friendship. Whatever else this is (and it is many-layered), this is a love feast. It is a meal shared by intimates where profound things can be said and communion experienced.

For myself I love the Eucharist. I love its mystery and its wonder: they bring me to my knees. 'Therefore we before him bending this great sacrament revere,' as Thomas Aquinas wrote in his great Corpus Christi hymn. That is important to me – venerating Christ in the Eucharist, recalling with awe the sacrifice of Calvary and handling the holy gifts with reverence. But I also want to recapture the sense of the Eucharist as the love feast, as a meal with Christ and his friends, as we experience the intimacy of eyes that meet across the table, the affection of those who readily embrace one another, sensing the arms of God around them. How often I yearn for every Eucharist to be a coming to table of Jesus' friends.

I believe Peter and his companions had that experience in the meals they shared with Jesus, and had it supremely on that night of heightened emotions after he had washed their feet. I believe Jesus wants us to have that experience in the Eucharist too. It is the same message as in the washing of feet. In the sharing of the Eucharist – and later, in the giving of his body and his blood – he is saying to each one of us, 'I am your friend. I offer you the intimacy of friendship. Become, or become more deeply, God's friend.'

Thus it is that, somewhere along the line, and often early on, the would-be follower of Jesus does well to discover the deep satisfaction, nourishment and joy that comes from sharing in the Eucharist, meeting Jesus in word, sacrament and fellowship, and being fed by the bread that becomes for us his body and the wine his blood. To be his companion, which is essential if we are to become his friend, means to eat with him, and indeed to eat with his many other companions. To be his companion is something Jesus longs for us to be. I suspect he is saddened by rules that make it more difficult. He is the hospitable Christ, always inviting others to the table, always wanting to share with those who want to draw close to him; he is not checking credentials, but is simply looking for signs of a relationship that might grow into friendship. 'Stretch out your hand,' he seems to be saying to those on pilgrimage and needing food for the journey, 'stretch out your hand and be fed by me.'

To those of us finding our way into a deeper relationship with him, a Jesus who desires our friendship and offers them his own, who looks for mutuality and cannot hide his vulnerability may sound rather intrusive, perhaps more than we can cope with. We cannot quite know where it might lead us. It might change a lot in our lives. A more contractual relationship, like that of a servant and his master, may be an easier option.

But a Jesus who desires our friendship and offers us his, who looks for mutuality and cannot hide vulnerability, may seem wonderfully attractive. It may speak to the deep longing in our heart. We may find ourselves saying, 'Yes, to really know his friendship – yes, to really be God's friend . . . yes, that's what I need above all else and I hadn't understood it.'

John, of course, only hints at what follows the supper. The other evangelists tell rather more, and once again Peter plays a key role. There is more to say about that. We shall discover that, as in the washing of feet and the sharing of the supper, so also in the going out into the darkness of the night, Jesus says to those who can hear it, 'I am your friend. I offer you the intimacy of friendship. Become, or become more deeply, God's friend.' At every stage as the Passion unfolds, it becomes clearer that the one thing truly worthwhile is to become God's friend.

5

Losing not a single one

The mood changes very quickly in John 13. Jesus has only just washed the disciples' feet and taught them something of the meaning of what he has done. His next words are about betrayal. They fit uneasily with the celebration of love and friendship that has just taken place in that little community. But denial and betrayal will dominate the next few hours in Peter's life. We who follow Jesus are aware how often denial and betrayal undermine our attempts to be disciples. What is remarkable, of course, is that, because of the unshakeable love of God, not a single person is lost through this denial and betrayal. Always there is the compassionate forgiveness of the crucified Lord.

We are still at the supper, though soon we will be in the garden and it will be dark. Picture the scene at the supper, if you will. It is a very familiar one. Jesus and his disciples are sharing the meal. Although perhaps not historically accurate, the picture that often comes into our mind's eye is Leonardo da Vinci's representation of the scene: the long table, Jesus at the centre, the disciples to either side, the Beloved Disciple leaning towards Jesus. But let me describe another painting, consciously drawing on da Vinci, but signalling something different. It is a contemporary painting by Lorna May Wadsworth and it is to be found over the altar in St George's Church, Nailsworth, Gloucestershire. It is a striking picture; some of the detail some people may find slightly shocking, though I suspect that many works of religious art that we now take for granted may have caused raised eyebrows when they were first unveiled.

When I first saw the painting, I struggled a little with one aspect of it. In recalling the event of the supper on the night before Jesus died, the artist focuses on a particular moment. The moment is the betrayal. Jesus and Judas Iscariot both have their hand in the dish. The Fourth Gospel describes the moment like this: Jesus, 'troubled in spirit' as the writer puts it, reveals to his disciples that one of them will betray him. The disciples, aghast, look at one another. Peter encourages one of the disciples, 'the one whom Jesus loved' and who is next to Jesus, to ask who it will be. Jesus replies that it will be the one to whom he gives a piece of bread that has been dipped in the dish. It is to Judas that he gives the bread, and we are told that this was the moment when Satan entered him. As he goes out, Jesus says to him, 'Do quickly what you are going to do' (John 13.21–27).

The reason I struggled a little with the Nailsworth painting was that I wasn't sure that, if I lived in Nailsworth, I would want, every time I came to kneel at the altar rail to receive communion, to be reminded either of Judas's betrayal, or even of my own. Of course, like everybody else, I have sometimes betrayed someone, or betrayed a trust, or even (and, I suppose, often) betrayed God. But I didn't want the people of Nailsworth always to be coming to communion weighed down by the knowledge and guilt of betrayal. I would rather focus, more positively, on what Jesus did at the supper, what he does at the Eucharist: feeds, nourishes, unfailingly gives in the bread and the wine a share in his risen life, as he does every time Christians come. From the way John 13 proceeds, I draw the further conclusion that Jesus himself would not want betrayal to be the focus of our thoughts, for the Fourth Gospel sets within a quite extraordinary framework the invitation to the betrayer to do quickly what he is going to do.

One moment Jesus is washing the disciples' feet and encouraging them to wash one another's feet – loving intimacy acted out. The next moment he is warning them that he is to be betrayed and speaks directly to the betrayer. And then, as soon as Judas has gone out into the night, Jesus says this:

> Now the Son of Man has been glorified, and God has been glorified in him. If God has been glorified in him, God will also glorify him in himself and will glorify him at once. Little children, I am with you only a little longer. You will look for me; and as I said to the Jews so now I say to you, 'Where I am going, you cannot come.' I give you a new commandment, that you love one another. By this everyone will know that you are my disciples, if you have love for one another. (John 13.31–35)

The conversation about betrayal has only just taken place. And then Jesus immediately says, 'I give you a new commandment, that you love one another.' Even at this moment – perhaps especially at this moment – his talk is of love. It is remarkable, isn't it? Though we shouldn't be surprised, knowing this is Jesus and it is entirely in line with his character. He is about to be betrayed, and he knows it, but his talk is not of bitterness or regret, but of love. Jesus still loves Judas. Jesus loves the betrayer.

Betrayal doesn't overcome God's love. Jesus just keeps loving and goes on urging the others to love. Perhaps he is wanting them to love Judas, as he does, betrayer or not. That betrayal doesn't overcome God's love is such an important and wonderful truth. Maybe the people in Nailsworth, and come to that the people in every church – maybe I myself – need when we come to the altar table to remember that we are betrayers. Those of us who call ourselves disciples, friends even, of Jesus, we are betrayers. Every day we betray someone or something. Most of our betrayals are small ones; they probably do not weigh us down with guilt or remorse. We fail to defend someone. We do not quite tell the whole truth. We stay silent when faith is scorned or justice denied. There may be bigger betrayals – most often we betray faithful relationships. Large or small, every day we are guilty of betrayal. But every day, unaffected by our betrayal, the food is put out for us and we are bidden to eat. Feeding is what God reliably does, despite our betrayal; he feeds, nourishes, offers a share in the life of the Risen Lord. God doesn't change his mind about us.

But here is another remarkable thing. After the talk of betrayal, Jesus speaks of love – and look what happens next. Jesus has only just uttered his words about love when Peter jumps in, the way Peter often does.

> Simon Peter said to him, 'Lord, where are you going?' Jesus answered, 'Where I am going, you cannot follow me now; but you will follow afterwards.' Peter said to him, 'Lord, why can I not follow you now? I will lay down my life for you.' Jesus answered, 'Will you lay down your life for me? Very truly, I tell you, before the cock crows, you will have denied me three times.'
> (John 13.36–38)

We have only just had the prediction of a betrayal and now we have the prediction of a denial. Peter, protesting his love, is nevertheless going to deny three times that he even knows Jesus, and it is to happen that very night. He has only just been invited to love and, within hours, he will have betrayed (for it is another kind of betrayal) his friend. It is remarkable that Jesus utters this passage of beautiful tenderness, inviting his disciples to love one another, between two warnings of betrayal. It isn't only Judas whom Jesus loves despite everything; it is Peter too. And of course, later, that love and Peter's response to it will be explored again by the lakeside at Easter, when three times Jesus will ask Peter, 'Do you love me?'

Let us return for a moment now to those unexpected words Jesus utters when Judas has gone out. Jesus speaks of love, but he also speaks of glory. He says, 'Now the Son of Man has been glorified, and God has been glorified in him.' We need to consider why Jesus speaks these words at this particular moment, just after Judas has been identified as a betrayer and before Peter's failure has been foretold. What has just happened in which Jesus has been glorified and God has been glorified in him?

What has just happened is that Jesus has been down on his knees washing the feet of his disciples. Could it be that the foot-washing is the way that Jesus has been glorified and God has been glorified in him? This messy, down-on-the-floor affair, with hot and sticky feet being tenderly bathed by Jesus in an act that looks a bit like service, and a bit like humility, but rather more like love, reveals the glory of Jesus and the glory of God. That is a wonderful challenge to conventional glory. The glory of God is Jesus on his knees with a bowl, a jug and a towel – what a thought! It is the acting out, the sacramental sign, of this unshakeable love of God, which is there for Judas and Peter and you and me. The foot-washing is the outward and visible sign of the inward and spiritual grace that emanates from a God whose character is to keep on loving, to keep on needing to show his extravagant love. It was Peter who found the foot-washing so challenging as he struggled with the idea of the master who had turned into an intimate, loving friend. Perhaps he could at least half see beyond the sign to an intimate loving God.

Jesus not only looks back, as he says 'the Son of Man has been glorified', but also looks forward to the immediate future. 'If God has been glorified in him, God *will* also glorify him in himself and will glorify him at once' (John 13.32; emphasis mine). What is the 'at once' to which he looks?

The very next thing is the time in the garden, the betrayal, the trial, the denial, the death on the cross. John certainly understood that as glory, but again it is the glory of the one who hangs naked, denied and betrayed by those who have fled, but with the divine loving still alive in him and being poured out from the cross on those who have the fortitude to stay – and surely, in pouring it out on them, to pour it out also on those who have fled. The loving was the glory of God.

But that is to jump ahead. For before we come to the cross itself, from which Peter will be absent, we need to look more closely at the events in the garden and the act of denial.

We need to return to Matthew's Gospel to be reminded how the synoptic writers describe what happened after supper in the garden. Jesus goes to the Garden of Gethsemane, taking his disciples, the ones who are meant to be his friends, with him. He puts some distance between the main body of disciples and Peter, James and John, who go a little further with him. Then, sharing with them his sense of grief and foreboding and urging them to stay awake, he leaves them also, moves on alone, throws himself to the ground and prays in a kind of spiritual agony to God, 'My Father, if it is possible, let this cup pass from me; yet not what I want but what you want.' He returns to the disciples. They are sleeping. It is to Peter in particular that he says, 'So, could you not stay awake with me one hour? Stay awake, and pray that you may not come into the time of trial; the spirit indeed is willing, but the flesh is weak.' Three times this happens – Jesus moves beyond them, prays his agonized prayer, comes back and finds them asleep. There is no fourth opportunity, for the party come to arrest him are close at hand. 'Are you still sleeping and taking your rest?' he says to them. 'See, the hour is at hand, and the

Son of Man is betrayed into the hands of sinners' (Matthew 26.36–45).

Once again Jesus is with Peter, James and John, the intimate circle that he has brought together before. They have seen him raise the dead. They have seen a vision of his future glory in the Transfiguration. Now they witness, or perhaps fail to witness, his intimacy with the Father and his vulnerability in the face of what lies ahead of him. For all that he is divine, this is a very human Jesus, needing his friends in his hour of need. It is natural that he should want them by his side, encouraging and upholding him. Such is their friendship that he is willing they should see into his heart and understand both his intimate trust in his Father and the grief that is taking hold of him. If only they could have kept awake.

If this is indeed an eyewitness report, they must have at least caught a glimpse of Jesus' agony, but soon they closed their eyes to it. They could not cope with it and allowed sleep to overcome them. This was betrayal too, even if they spoke no word of denial. And there is a kind of irony in the words of Jesus to Peter that he should pray not to come to the time of trial. It has echoes, of course, of the Lord's Prayer, which has already shaped the words Jesus speaks to his Father. And the time of trial was indeed only just around the corner for Peter, and he was to fail the test, though one day, as Jesus would later predict, Peter would face another time of trial and this time be faithful.

Unlike Matthew, Mark and Luke, the Fourth Gospel only hints at what follows the supper. There is no agony in the garden, with a sleeping Peter, James and John – only a Jesus who says with confidence, 'Shall I not drink the cup that the Father has given me?' But, even as John tells it (18.7–11), it is in the dark of the night that they come to arrest Jesus and even John cannot hide entirely the moment of fear, foreboding and failure. It is a dramatic moment as the soldiers come with their lanterns and torches and weapons. Even at this point Peter, denial only minutes away, has a role. He has a sword and he draws it. He strikes out at Malchus, a slave of the high priest, and cuts off his ear. But Jesus will have none of it. 'Put your sword back into its sheath. Am I not to drink the cup that the Father has given me?'

Here is Peter, as always wanting to do the right thing and, as so often, getting it wrong. It is a meaningless, pointless gesture, Peter with his sword against a detachment of soldiers. It shows fierce loyalty, courage (the last such moment for a while), perhaps even love, but it also reveals a profound misunderstanding. Jesus has been preparing the disciples for his Passion ever since Peter called him Messiah. Over and over again he has tried to help them understand. But still Peter is unable to accept that Jesus must drink the cup that the Father has given him. He is still setting his mind on human things, not on divine things, just as at Caesarea Philippi when Jesus heard in his words the temptation of Satan (Matthew 16.23). But note the words of Jesus in John 18.9, 'I did not lose a single one of those whom you gave me.' It is a reference back to John 17.12, where Jesus says in his prayer to the Father, 'Not one of them was lost except the one destined to be lost' – by which he must mean Satan, rather than Judas. For all that Peter is getting everything wrong, indeed frustrating the path Jesus is following, he is not going to be lost. The love that Jesus has been talking about will still encompass him. And Judas too – not a single one will be lost.

Jesus is arrested, bound and taken for trial. It only remains for Peter to act out what Jesus has said will take place. It happens all too soon, just as Jesus has said, and is a failure of discipleship and of friendship as complete as could be.

Simon Peter and another disciple followed Jesus. Since that disciple was known to the high priest, he went with Jesus into the courtyard of the high priest, but Peter was standing outside at the gate. So the other disciple, who was known to the high priest, went out, spoke to the woman who guarded the gate, and brought Peter in. The woman said to Peter, 'You are not also one of this man's disciples, are you?' He said, 'I am not.' Now the slaves and the police had made a charcoal fire because it was cold, and they were standing round it and warming themselves. Peter also was standing with them and warming himself . . .

They asked him, 'You are not also one of his disciples, are you?' He denied it and said, 'I am not.' One of the slaves of the high priest, a relative of the man whose ear Peter had cut off, asked, 'Did I not see you in the garden with him?' Again Peter denied it, and at that moment the cock crowed.

(John 18.15–18, 25b–27)

John is remarkably restrained. Only by his repeated use of the word 'disciple' in this short passage does he emphasize what is happening – the disciple is no longer following, but is denying, betraying and deserting; he is walking away from his discipleship. John tells us nothing of Peter's feelings at this moment. Perhaps he imagines it will take Peter longer to understand what he has done. The other Gospel writers tell us more – how, realizing what he had done, he wept bitterly. It is Luke who expresses, through mention of a simple gesture, the sense of betrayal. 'The Lord turned and looked at Peter', Luke recounts. It is at that moment that Peter remembers Jesus' words about how he would deny Jesus three times. It is that look that brings on his bitter tears (Luke 22.60b–62).

If Jesus did indeed turn and look at Peter, we may wonder what his eyes conveyed. Disappointment perhaps, probably not rebuke. If everything we have discovered about Jesus is true, then he will have looked at Peter with eyes of love. After all, as John tells it, a discourse about love was the context in which he spoke of Judas' betrayal and Peter's denial. Not a single one was to be lost. Of course the experience of Judas and that of Peter are different. Judas simply cannot cope with the extravagant love that is on offer and has to remove it from the scene. Peter, on the other hand, while clumsy in his responses and later fearful, wants to keep working towards the acceptance of that extravagant love, desiring it deeply.

We recognize these moments of betrayal. For at times in our lives, like Peter and James and John in the garden, we let down Jesus our friend. Like Peter in the courtyard, we deny Jesus our friend. Like the whole company of the disciples, we desert our friend, we walk away. We are not sure we want to be the friend of God.

The cares of this world, or the sense that this relationship carries too much risk of turning our world upside down, will have us walk away. But even here, the story of Peter assures us, there is good news. For Christ will take our selfishness, our fear, our heart of stone, our sin and carry it with his cross to the hill outside the city. He will allow himself to be nailed to that cross and, looking down from it, will say to you, as he says to me, 'No one has greater love than this, to lay down one's life for one's friends. You are my friends' (John 15.13). Even though you are hiding, even though you have abandoned me, you are my friends.

For those of us who want to follow Jesus, there are many lessons here to learn. We need to grasp a difficult truth about ourselves and be honest about it. We are guilty of betrayal. In all sorts of ways we are guilty of betrayal. We need to understand a wonderful truth about the God we meet in Jesus. God's love is unshakeable, dependable, unconditional. Betrayal does not overcome it. Every day God goes on feeding, nourishing, inviting us to the table, where he gives us a share in the risen life of Jesus. We need to see in the talk of love and glory and in the beautiful, tender act of love we call the foot-washing a compelling picture of inward grace, of the intimate loving God who invites us into his life.

In the middle of that dark night, Peter could not see that. All he could do was weep bitterly.

6

For he was naked

———•◦•———

There are not many stories told by all four Gospel writers. But they all recount Peter's denial, and Matthew, Mark and Luke all end their description of this event with the picture of Peter weeping. The Fourth Gospel, more reticent, simply notes that the cock crowed. And then, when it comes to Peter, there is silence. He is simply not mentioned again until Jesus is dead and buried and two days have passed.

If it is always dangerous to try to synthesize the versions of stories given in different Gospels, it is all the more dangerous when it comes to the evangelists' treatment of the resurrection. Each seems to be seeking words for the indescribable and the mystical. The Jesus who has been raised comes and goes, relating to the disciples in a quite different way from his life with them before his Passion. And each appearance stands as a moment of revelation and grace somehow independent of the others, resisting any attempt to be drawn into a coherent and developing story. Where Simon Peter fits into it all is equally difficult to determine. In this chapter I maintain that the key to the restoration of Peter's relationship with Jesus comes in John 21. But first we must examine some other texts for clues.

Mark's engagement with the resurrection is brief and mysterious, all of it expressed in just eight verses and ending, so to speak, in mid-air. There is a single verse that refers to Peter; 'Go, tell his disciples and Peter that he is going ahead of you to Galilee; there you will see him, just as he told you' (16.7).

How are we to understand this first mention of Peter since he went out weeping bitterly? Is he specifically named simply because he is so often the disciples' leader and spokesperson? Perhaps so, though Mark makes less of that role than others. Is it a coded message to Peter that, despite his denial, he is still the disciple and friend of Jesus, the very naming of him a kind of restoration? Perhaps. Or is it, as some commentators have suggested, a sign that Peter has separated himself from the disciples? That Peter, broken by his betrayal, has walked away, no longer thinking of himself as a disciple and therefore needing to be called back into relationship, not only with Jesus, but with the community of disciples? Of course we cannot know the answer, but to picture a Peter who feels entirely alienated by his denial is to recognize a depth of despair or grief that we ourselves sometimes feel, whether in our relationship with God or with human beings, one that cries out for something quite big and significant to bring healing and restore wholeness.

Interestingly, Matthew, who so often wants to give Peter prominence, simply says in his equivalent verse that the women were to tell the disciples (28.7). There is no mention of Peter. From Matthew's perspective, he may not have wanted to over-emphasize the thought of an alienated Peter. Matthew's Peter might have denied Jesus, but he would not have walked away entirely.

Luke is full of interest for us. The women go to the tomb on Easter morning, receive the message from the 'two men in dazzling clothes', whom we must take to be angels, and return to tell the disciples the news. The disciples regard this as an 'idle', we might say 'unlikely' tale and do not believe them (Luke

24.1–11). Peter alone, believing or not, is inspired to respond to their story. 'But Peter got up and ran to the tomb,' Luke records. 'Stooping and looking in, he saw the linen cloths by themselves; then he went home, amazed at what had happened' (24.12).

It is a far shorter and less complex version of the story than the Fourth Gospel will tell. It is not a resurrection appearance of the Lord to Peter, but it suggests a longing on Peter's part to find Jesus. It does not indicate belief that Jesus has been raised, but it does record amazement. What is interesting is how it ties in with a verse later in the chapter, when Luke writes 'They [the Eleven and their companions] were saying, "The Lord has risen indeed, and he has appeared to Simon"' (24.34).

This is said in response to the tale that the two from Emmaus were able to tell about how the Lord, unrecognized, walked with them and went in to have supper with them, and how they recognized him at the breaking of the bread. Returning to Jerusalem, elated by this encounter, they discover that the apostles too have accepted that Jesus has been raised because he has appeared to Simon. It is fascinating, of course, that the account reverts to the name 'Simon', as if the apostles are not quite sure that Simon is, at this moment, the rock that Jesus said he would be. But it is more fascinating that it refers to an appearance to Peter, presumably alone, that is not recounted in any of the Gospels. Paul, in 1 Corinthians 15.5, listing a number of resurrection appearances, also says that Jesus appeared 'to Cephas', but gives no detail. We simply do not know any detail of this appearance, but Luke describes it as happening on Easter Day itself. It is the last mention of Peter in Luke's Gospel, though Peter will, of course, feature prominently in the sequel, the Acts of the Apostles. An assertion of an appearance to Peter is perhaps Luke's way of affirming Peter's restoration, which the Fourth Gospel will describe much more fully.

* * *

In John's Gospel, like Luke's, it is a woman who goes first to the tomb 'early on the first day of the week'. In John there is only one woman, Mary Magdalene, and she sees the stone rolled away but encounters no angels. She runs to Simon Peter and 'the other disciple, the one Jesus loved' with the news that 'they have taken the Lord out of the tomb and we do not know where they have laid him' (John 20.1–2). The account continues with Peter and the other disciple running to the tomb. Peter is unable to keep up with his companion, who reaches the tomb first but waits outside. When Peter arrives he goes in, sees the linen wrappings that had been bound around Jesus and the cloth that would have been wrapped around his head. The other disciple joins him and we are told that they did not yet understand the Scripture that he must rise from the dead, but that other disciple 'saw and believed' (John 20.3–10).

Sometimes this passage is described in terms of a competitive race, and certainly there is in the Gospel stories a tension between the two disciples. But the running is not so much about outdoing one another, but about a longing to leave behind the despair of the last hours and to reconnect with Jesus. The way that one and then the other takes the lead, one pressing forward, one hesitating or holding back, is not so much a competition as a description of how discipleship often works: we move forward together, often in dialogue with someone who is walking the same way with us, but not always at exactly the same speed or with exactly the same expectations. We help each other along, encourage one another, force or decrease the pace. Discipleship often deepens through such friendships, and we are wise if we have people who will walk (and just occasionally run) with us. And that is what is happening to Peter and the Beloved Disciple as they penetrate the mystery of the empty tomb. They also act out, in this pilgrimage to the tomb, stages of faith. They set out with a lack of belief in Mary's report, move forward into partial faith, at a speed with which they can cope, and then go on towards a full faith, seeing and believing. At least that is where the Beloved Disciple arrives before they go home. The evangelist does not say as much of Peter.

For the rest of John 20, sometimes regarded as the original end of the Gospel, Peter is not mentioned by name. Mary Magdalene meets Jesus in the garden (20.11–18), Jesus appears twice to the disciples in the upper room – the first time with Thomas absent, the second when he is present and makes his great profession of faith, 'My Lord and my God' (20.19–29). Peter is present, presumably, on both occasions. But we are not told so. That constitutes one of the strongest reasons for believing that John 21, for all that it does not seem to flow from the rest of John and reads like an independent account of the Easter experience, is an authentic part of the original Gospel, an epilogue rather than a later addition or a postscript. Without it we are left with a Peter who has entered the tomb, but has not encountered the one who has left the grave clothes behind and come out. Scholars continue to explore the relationship between the two chapters. It is difficult to make sense of disciples who have been reunited with Jesus in the upper room, have acknowledged him, in Thomas's words, as 'Lord and God', have received the Holy Spirit, simply going back to Galilee and to their fishing. But this is where we have to resist the desire to create a coherent story; instead we must be satisfied with glimpses of the experience of living with a risen Jesus, who comes and goes and surprises us. For Peter, what we find in John 21 is key.

The first 19 verses of John 21 take us through three connected scenes in a story of huge significance. In the first scene Simon Peter invites his friends to go with him on a night-time fishing expedition; we see them out on the lake, but they catch nothing. In the second scene the boat comes to the shore and the disciples are reunited with Jesus, who has breakfast prepared for them and invites them to eat; it has the atmosphere of the Eucharist. Finally, with everyone else fading into the background, there is a dialogue of immense beauty and sensitivity between Jesus and Simon Peter, with its exchange, repeated three times, 'Do you love me? Feed my sheep.'

Seven of the disciples are gathered together and Peter suggests they go fishing. They do this, but despite fishing all night, they catch nothing. It is reminiscent of the fishing expedition described in Luke 5, when Peter first becomes a disciple. The day has just dawned when Jesus, standing on the beach, calls to the men in the boat, asking about their catch. He urges them to cast the net to the right side. They do so and make a spectacular catch, too many fish to haul in the net. And then there is a moment of recognition.

> That disciple whom Jesus loved said to Peter, 'It is the Lord!' When Simon Peter heard it was the Lord, he put on some clothes, for he was naked, and jumped into the sea. But the other disciples came in the boat, dragging the net full of fish, for they were not far from land, only about a hundred yards off.
>
> (John 21.7–8)

There are many angles from which to approach this story. We might put the emphasis on the amazing catch of fish. We might spend some time trying to work out whether 153 – the number of fish that they dragged back to shore in the net – is significant. We might focus on the meal of bread and fish on the beach. With John the evangelist every line is significant; everything has its meaning.

Or we might wonder at the remarkable similarities with the story we encountered in Chapter 1 – Luke's account of how

Simon Peter was drawn into discipleship at the beginning of his story. In Luke Jesus gave the advice to 'put out into deep water and let down your nets for a catch' (5.4); in John he says, 'Cast the net on the right side of the boat and you will find some' (21.6). The advice on both occasions is sound. 'When they had done this, they caught so many fish that their nets were beginning to break' (Luke 5.6); 'They were not able to haul it in because there were so many fish' (John 21.6). There is also Peter's repentance. In Luke his response to the miraculous catch was one that recognized his sinfulness: 'Go away from me, Lord, for I am a sinful man,' he says. In the lakeside exchange in John 21 the issue is his denial. Each time sinfulness or failure are not the end of things. Each time he hears the invitation to follow. Scholars, and not only scholars, wonder whether Luke took what is essentially a resurrection story, and transferred it to the beginning of Jesus' ministry in order to show that what brought Peter to faith was his witness to what God had done in Jesus. But by the lake after the resurrection is where it really belongs.

For I do believe this story is essentially about the restoration of Peter's relationship with Jesus. And the words that really make me think are these: 'When Simon Peter heard it was the Lord, he put on some clothes, for he was naked' (21.7).

'He put on some clothes, for he was naked.' Why ever does John give us that detail? I've thought about that very hard. There are scholars who will explain it away and paraphrase it as something like 'he tucked in his outer garment', but the plain meaning, surprising of course, is that 'he was naked'. And this is the Fourth Gospel, where every word is significant and has a meaning beyond the obvious. I've found myself drawn back to another story where people are naked and feel a need to cover up. In Genesis 3 we read:

When the woman saw that the tree was good for food, and that it was a delight to the eyes, and that the tree was to be desired to make one wise, she took of its fruit and ate; and she also gave some to her husband, who was with her, and he ate. Then the eyes of both were opened, and they knew that they were naked; and they sewed fig leaves together and made loincloths for themselves.

They heard the sound of the Lord God walking in the garden at the time of the evening breeze, and the man and his wife hid themselves from the presence of the Lord God among the trees of the garden. But the Lord God called to the man, and said to him, 'Where are you?' He said, 'I heard the sound of you in the garden, and I was afraid, because I was naked; and I hid myself.'

(Genesis 3.6–10)

What we are seeing in that beautiful, poetic account of humanity's fall is how the relationship of Adam and Eve with God has been destroyed by their disobedience. Shame comes into their lives and shame makes them aware of their nakedness. They need to clothe themselves – in loincloths made of fig leaves – to hide their shame before they can face God and engage with him about what they have done. Indeed their deeper fall from grace is not in their disobedience, but in their hiding from God, their attempt to renege on relationship with him. The result of their meeting with their creator, naked save for the fig leaves they have made, is their banishment from the garden and the great divide between God and his creation that we call the fall.

It is not difficult to see the parallel. Perhaps it accounts for John's inclusion of the apparently unimportant detail that Peter stopped to hide his nakedness. Adam and Eve have been alienated from God by their disobedience, eating of the fruit that God told them not to eat. Peter has been alienated from Jesus by his denial, back on Maundy Thursday, when three times, asked whether he was one of the disciples of Jesus, he denied it, denied his friend, denied and fled. Shame comes into the lives of Adam and Eve. Shame comes into Peter's life as the cock crows and he remembers the words of Jesus, 'Before the cock crows twice, you will deny me three times.' And Jesus turns and looks at Peter, who is overwhelmed with shame and goes outside and weeps bitterly.

Shame makes Adam and Eve aware of their nakedness. They don't know how they can face God in the vulnerability of their exposure, their nakedness, and so they search for covering. As soon as that is done, they hear the sound of the Lord God, walking in the garden and engaging with them in a way that exposes their disobedience and their sin.

In our story of Peter, it is the Beloved Disciple, Peter's friend – though, it sometimes seems, also his rival for the affection of Jesus – who suddenly realizes that the figure on the beach is none other than Jesus. It is Jesus who has directed them where to find the catch of fish. It is Jesus beckoning them to come ashore. It is Jesus cooking the breakfast on the charcoal fire. 'It is the Lord!' he exclaims – John who always gets there first, as he did on Easter morning when he outran Peter to the tomb. Peter, hearing that, wants to go to Jesus, so he jumps overboard and swims to the shore, wanting to get there first, ahead of the others in the boat dragging the net to land. But first he must hide his shame, clothe his nakedness, so that he does not come to the Lord entirely vulnerable, utterly exposed. He must come to Jesus clothed.

So Peter comes to Jesus, with all that unresolved tension arising from his denial, with all the shame, with all the foreboding. Will he too be banished? Will his fall from grace be permanent? And, like God in the garden with Adam and Eve, Jesus on the shore of the lake brings the issue into the open, and he does it through a question.

> When they had finished breakfast, Jesus said to Simon Peter, 'Simon son of John, do you love me more than these?' He said to him, 'Yes, Lord; you know that I love you.' Jesus said to him, 'Feed my lambs.' A second time he said to him, 'Simon son of John, do you love me?' He said to him, 'Yes, Lord; you know that I love you.' Jesus said to him, 'Tend my sheep.' He said to him the third time, 'Simon son of John, do you love me?' Peter felt hurt because he said to him the third time, 'Do you love me?' And he said to him, 'Lord, you know everything; you know that I love you.' Jesus said to him, 'Feed my sheep.'

(John 21.15–17)

Jesus brings the issue of Peter's denial out into the open in order that he may resolve it. He needs to help Peter let the shame go. He wants to draw Peter back into friendship. There is to be no banishment. Reconciliation is the intention.

The English translations of the Greek do not bring out that, in this exchange about love, two different words are used. In the first two questions, the Greek is *agapao*. In all three of Peter's replies, and in Jesus' third question, the Greek is *phileo*. Both are quite properly translated 'love' and many scholars play down the significance, reminding us that it was the practice of the writer of the Fourth Gospel to use synonymous verbs for stylistic variety. I am not convinced. The change the third time Jesus asks his question, against the absolute consistency of Peter's reply, must be significant. A number of commentators, as far back as William Temple in *Readings in St John's Gospel* (1947), have found it helpful to translate *phileo* in terms of friendship. 'Simon, son of John, do you love me?' Jesus asks twice, and both times Peter replies, 'Yes, Lord, you know that I am your friend.' The third time Jesus adopts Peter's word. 'Simon, son of John, are you my friend?' And Peter gives the same answer.

What is going on here? The first time Jesus actually asks, 'Do you love me more than these?' And for all the lack of condemnation in the question, it will have struck Peter, who claimed at the supper that even if everybody else fell away he would be faithful, that there is no way now that he can say he loves Jesus more than the others. His betrayal has been the worst. But he can say that he loves him, even if not more than the others, or he can say something almost the same, that he is his friend. The second time, Jesus sticks with a question about love and gets from Peter a second answer about friendship. Then Jesus comes into line and asks Peter whether he is his friend. The writer tells us that Peter was hurt that Jesus asked him the third time whether he was his friend. Was that because Jesus had changed the word, or was it simply that Peter was hurt that the question kept on being put? Or was it that, in that moment, he finally understood that the threefold questioning was intended to address the unresolved issue of his threefold denial?

I do think people usually interpret 'friend' as a weaker word than 'love', as if Jesus and Peter were opting for something easier and less intimate. I think they are wrong, and such an understanding would not be true to Scripture. Remember Gregory of Nyssa: 'the one thing truly worthwhile is becoming God's friend'. When he urges that, he is only reflecting Scripture and in particular the actions and words of Jesus himself, spoken on Maundy Thursday, only hours before the huge failure of friendship in Peter's denial.

We have explored how, in John 13, there in the upstairs room the night before he dies, Jesus washes the feet of his disciples, prominent among them Peter, who at first copes with it badly. He resists the intimacy of a Jesus who gets down on his knees to wash Peter's feet, though he comes to realize the beauty of what Jesus is doing and says, 'not my feet only, but also my hands and my head' – 'all of me'. And just in case they mistake the act for a simple one of service or humility, Jesus makes it absolutely clear that it was the action of a friend, an action shaped by love, when he says a little later: 'This is my commandment, that you love one another as I have loved you. No one has greater love than this, to lay down one's life for one's friends. You are my friends if you do what I command you' (John 15.12–14).

So – far from friendship being something less than love – by assuring Jesus that he is his friend Peter is making the connection with the night of Maundy Thursday, recognizing that his denial followed on so soon from the friendship expressed in the washing of the disciples' feet and asking for their friendship to be restored. And Jesus with his repeated, 'Feed my lambs, tend my sheep', is restoring Peter as disciple and friend. Indeed the exchange ends with the same words that Jesus first addressed to him on the lakeside when he called him to discipleship three years before. 'Follow me,' he says now as he did then. It is a fresh start, a new creation. And somehow in that intense and searching dialogue between Jesus and Peter we sense that, clothes or no clothes, Peter has at last allowed himself to express his vulnerability and the intimacy of his love, his friendship, for this Lord, to whom he is utterly devoted – for whom, in his better moments, he is willing to die. And die he will, as Jesus says to him:

'Very truly, I tell you, when you were younger, you used to fasten your own belt and to go wherever you wished. But when you grow old, you will stretch out your hands, and someone else will fasten a belt around you and take you where you do not wish to go.' (He said this to indicate the kind of death by which he would glorify God.) After this he said to him, 'Follow me.' (John 21.18–19)

It is a wonderfully rich story of reversal, reconciliation and resurrection. In the reversal of Peter's threefold denial in a threefold commission, in the reconciliation of Peter with his friend, in the resurrection of Peter, a mirroring of Jesus' resurrection, as Peter is raised from the death of sin and shame and clothed in the new life of the resurrection, we are given a glimpse of what the Risen Lord offers to the human race and to each one of us.

Jesus offers the world for all time, he guarantees for all time, the reversal of the fall that banished us from the garden of God's delight. He restores the human race to paradise. He invites us back into the sphere of God's grace.

Jesus holds out to us his hand of friendship. He wants to be our friend. He wants us to be the friends of God. He wants us to know that, like him and with him, like him and like God, we can come to him naked, so to speak, with no pretence for covering, with no need to hide in shame, with every reason to let our vulnerability show and not to be afraid.

Jesus clothes us in robes of resurrection. Within their folds are light and life and joy and love. Like a coat of many colours given by a loving Father, like a festal garment thrown around the shoulders of a prodigal son whose return fills his father with delight, God in Christ clothes us in robes of resurrection and invites us to be daily more and more alive with his risen life.

7

Filled with the Holy Spirit

————•◦•————

Peter, though he has denied Jesus, has been reunited with his Lord and restored as disciple and friend. If we pick up Peter's story in the Acts of the Apostles, he is very much back at the centre of the community and once again its spokesman. He is also very much the mature disciple, with much to teach us about the action of the Holy Spirit in those who follow Jesus, about living the resurrection life and about finding our place in the community of believers. We shall see in this chapter – and it is wonderful to see it – how a confident Peter, who knows himself to be a friend of God, is able to live in the strength of his Lord. It is the way a disciple wants to live.

The first mention of Peter by name in the Acts of the Apostles is in the upper room as the disciples await the promised Holy Spirit. But this is preceded in Acts by a dialogue between Jesus and his disciples and then by his return to the Father; Peter is not named here, but the clear implication is that he is present. He therefore reaches a new point in his relationship with Jesus. For the physical Jesus is being withdrawn as he goes back to the Father. Luke describes it in a remarkably literal way: 'As they were watching, he was lifted up, and a cloud took him out of their sight' (Acts 1.10–11).

This is probably poetic language for a transformation almost impossible to put into words. This has been a friendship based on a relationship of 'flesh and blood'. It was a Jesus with strong arms who lifted Peter out of the water, a Jesus with loving eyes who looked upon him on the night of trial, a Jesus with a familiar voice inviting, teaching and even rebuking. But that stage of the friendship is over. Peter will not again see in the flesh those arms or eyes; will not, other than in his imagination, hear that voice – at least not in this life. Friendships do, of course, survive – more than survive, flourish – without physical presence or touch. There is a quality of communion to them that can overcome physical absence, geographical distance and even long silences. For Peter it becomes like that, but the way he will speak and write of Jesus in the years that follow will be evidence that his closeness to Jesus and relationship with God grow deeper and stronger.

It is harder for us; we have not had that extraordinary privilege of knowing Jesus in the flesh. The First Letter of Peter addresses this difficulty when it says, 'Although you have not seen him, you love him; and even though you do not see him now, you believe in him and rejoice with an indescribable and glorious joy' (1 Peter 1.8). There are echoes here of Jesus' own words to Thomas, 'Blessed are those who have not seen and yet have come to believe' (John 20.29). To be a disciple of Jesus Christ is to cultivate a friendship with the one we cannot see, but whose presence we might sense in such a way that we all but see and touch and hear him.

I say 'might sense', for that is not the experience of all. Having a sense of a Jesus so close that you can almost touch him is a wonderful grace for those who have it. It comes, of course, partly by the exercise of the imagination, by living over and over again the Gospel stories, by entering so deeply the experience of Jesus that, yes, he might be at your side. You wouldn't be surprised if he was there beside you, a companion whose hand you could take into yours. But this sense of Jesus is not essential to Christian discipleship; indeed it is unusual. Certainly it is unusual as a steady state, although quite a few Christians have witnessed to particular and rare moments when they could speak of seeing Jesus. Seeing Jesus, however, is not what discipleship is about. Peter, for all that he knew the Jesus who walked this earth for 33 years and knew him 'in the flesh', seems to have grown in his faith in Jesus and in his love for Jesus in the years after Jesus ceased to be physically part of his world. Knowing the Christ who is set free from earthly limitations is, in the end, a greater blessing than knowing a Jesus constrained by time and space.

Returning from the mountain of the ascension, the disciples, including the 11 apostles and Mary the mother of Jesus, assemble in the upper room where they are staying. The apostles are listed; Peter is first among them, followed by John, the two in a new partnership that will keep them together through the significant events of the following chapters. Here they constantly devote themselves to prayer. There is expectancy in the air and they do not have to wait long, only the few days until Pentecost, for something dramatic and life-changing to happen. They later found this difficult to describe: the nearest they could get was to say that it sounded like a violent wind coming from heaven, filling the house in which they were gathered. It seemed as if there were flames, like fire, settling on each of them. Difficult as it was to find the words to describe the experience, what it meant to them was crystal clear. This was the promised Holy Spirit, for whom they had been waiting. Nor was the outcome hard to describe. They began to speak in a variety of languages that would communicate their message to those gathered from many nations in the city (Acts 2.1–11).

The promised Holy Spirit has come upon them – the entire community, not just the apostles – in a dramatic way, and people from a wide range of cultures and speaking a variety of languages are able to understand what they are saying. Their first words are unrecorded, but soon there is a clear spokesman and, almost inevitably, it is Peter. Drawing on the Hebrew Scriptures, the prophet Joel and the Psalms, he speaks about the Holy Spirit and proclaims the resurrection, giving his witness to Jesus.

> This man, handed over to you according to the definite plan and foreknowledge of God, you crucified and killed by the hands of those outside the law. But God raised him up, having freed him from death, because it was impossible for him to be held in its power. (Acts 2.23–24)

It is powerful preaching, effective too. For those who hear him are 'cut to the heart', want to respond, and they are baptized, three thousand of them on that day of Pentecost (Acts 2.37–41). Once baptized, they find themselves not left alone with their repentance and their new-found faith, but drawn into a community. It is the same community Jesus formed and of which Peter has been part, but now it is much larger; now it is a company of those who have been changed by the Holy Spirit. They are a company living a very particular sort of community life. Possessions are sold, the profit from the sales given to those in need, all things are held in common. Together they go to the temple, spending much time there. They eat together. They 'broke bread at home', which maybe is an early sign of sharing in the Eucharist. They enjoy the goodwill of those around them. This community is good news. It draws others in by the vibrancy of its common life. Acts tells us that, perhaps unsurprisingly, 'day by day the Lord added to their number those who were being saved' (2.47).

We need to explore what marks of discipleship can be found in this community, led by Peter, for these marks still have application for people as they respond to the gospel today. There are four such marks. The first is witness to the resurrection.

'This Jesus God raised up,' says Peter to the crowd on Pentecost Day, 'and of that all of us are witnesses' (Acts 2.32). For Peter and the other 11 apostles, this witness was to the raising of the one they had known in the flesh. But witness to the resurrection is part of the calling of every disciple and, because Jesus is, as Paul puts it, 'the first fruits of the harvest of the dead' (1 Corinthians 15.23), he is the exemplar of God's ongoing work of creating new life out of death. In a sense Peter in his very self was witness of resurrection. His denial and restoration were a little death and resurrection. And to witness to the resurrection is to be able to give witness to the activity of God in one's own life and in the lives of those around one. Very often coming to the new life of faith is itself a story of resurrection. Part of being a disciple is to discover within oneself, and to become articulate in describing, how the pattern of God's activity we see in Jesus is simply the way God is and the way God acts, in each one of us.

It's good to stop and ask oneself sometimes, 'How has resurrection happened in me?' People too easily associate resurrection simply with what happens to us when we die, even though, of course, what happens when we die is very different from what happened on the first Easter Day. Resurrection is as much part of life on earth as it is of life after we die. We will not always recognize what is happening to us as resurrection, but that is what it is, because a God whose very nature is to raise up is working on us and in us. We are deeply hurt, for instance, by the break-up of a long and deep personal relationship – with a close friend or a partner, maybe a marriage even – and for a while, perhaps a long while, we live, or at least exist, in a dark place, hoping for some light at the end of the tunnel, but hardly able to believe that we will flourish again. But gradually – or sometimes dramatically – by the grace of God, we so to speak come back to life. That's resurrection, and it is like coming back from the dead. Peter knew all about that. Because of what happened at the lakeside after the great catch of fish, Peter knew what he was talking about when it came to experiencing resurrection. It is a mark of the disciple.

The second mark is an openness to the Holy Spirit. Peter is clear that the extraordinary phenomenon of the Day of Pentecost is the work of the Spirit, that his own articulate preaching happens under the influence of the Spirit and that the gift of the Holy Spirit will come to those baptized in response to his preaching. For some in our own day the Holy Spirit comes in much the same way as at Pentecost – dramatically, turning people around, changing lives overnight, making them different people. When that happens, it is a cause of great joy and gratitude. But the indwelling and abiding of the Spirit is not always – perhaps not often – like that, as if God had only one way of giving the Spirit. More often we know that the Holy Spirit has made a home among us simply because we find we have gifts that we know are not of our making. Or we discover within ourselves fruits of love, joy and peace that surprise and delight us. Or we are amazed, as Peter must have been at Pentecost, to discover that something has loosened our tongue and enabled us to speak with new confidence about the faith that is in us. Or we are led into prayer in a way that is deeper than we had thought possible. All these are signs of the Holy Spirit at work within us, making us more truly disciples of Jesus and friends of God.

The third mark is a willingness to engage with the discipline of prayer. Prayer is not always a discipline – sometimes it is spontaneous praise, joy and longing. But in most lives it is, a good deal of the time, something of a discipline. It is significant that, in the Gospels, although the disciples are heard asking Jesus to teach them to pray, more often Jesus prays alone. In a sense the disciples did not have the same need to pray that we do, for they had Jesus there among them. They were able to relate to him in that way. But for those who have not seen Jesus, but who nevertheless love him, prayer is crucial in maintaining and deepening the relationship. So, as soon as Jesus has returned to the Father, the apostles' prayer becomes vital for all that follows. They pray in the upstairs room as they wait for Pentecost. They pray, at Peter's direction, for wisdom in choosing a replacement for Judas. They pray in the community that emerges from Pentecost. It is a mark of their shared discipleship.

They witness to the resurrection, they are open to the Holy Spirit, they engage with the discipline of prayer: these are three marks of the mature disciple, and Peter exemplifies all three. You would expect to find these three in anyone seeking to be God's friend. They do all of these within a community life, and that is the fourth mark of the mature disciple, that discipleship is lived out with all the delights, but also the tensions, of a community. There is in Acts no solitary Christian. The apostles' first reaction to the ascension is to gather together. Their choosing of a new apostle is to restore the apostolic community to its proper shape. Their experience of the outpouring of the Spirit is communal. The life into which they are called is all about fellowship, breaking bread together, sharing prayer time, holding goods in common.

The Christian community can be a difficult setting in which to be a disciple. For all that the Church is, in the words of an old prayer, a 'wonderful and sacred mystery', it can also be a tough community in which to live, dragged down by all the failings of fallen humanity, sometimes apparently happier dying slowly, stuck in its old ways, than following Jesus into an adventurous future brimming with fresh life. Although the Acts of the Apostles, with its ideal picture and its talk of those who believed being 'of one heart and soul', with great grace being upon them all (Acts 4.32–33), makes it sound as if, in the beginning, all was sweetness and light as believers lived the common life and won the goodwill of all, the letters of both Peter and Paul reveal that, right from the start, there were tensions and difficulties. But, challenging as it often is, the call to discipleship is a call into community, or, better still, into communion. Peter, who had been with Jesus from the beginning, knew that was what was involved.

So there quickly emerges around Peter and the apostles a growing community, where witness to the resurrection, openness to the Holy Spirit and a discipline of prayer are establishing themselves. Very soon this embryo church is to face the challenge of opposition. It is a popular movement, growing and making converts, and soon the goodwill shown towards it will dissipate, at least among the ruling religious class who will be threatened by it, and especially by miraculous signs.

Just such a sign is given when Peter and John, entering the temple at the time of afternoon prayer, encounter a lame man begging at the Beautiful Gate. He calls out to the two apostles hoping for money:

> Peter looked intently at him, as did John, and said, 'Look at us.' And he fixed his attention on them, expecting to receive something from them. But Peter said, 'I have no silver or gold, but what I have I give you; in the name of Jesus Christ of Nazareth, stand up and walk.' And he took him by the right hand and raised him up; and immediately his feet and ankles were made strong. Jumping up, he stood and began to walk, and he entered the temple with them, walking and leaping and praising God.
>
> (Acts 3.4–8)

'He took him by the hand and raised him up' – it is another little resurrection, another moment of life-giving by the One whose nature is to raise up. The people praise God, filled with wonder and amazement. Peter grasps the opportunity to address the crowd and presses home his message that this healing is in the name of Jesus, whom they killed, but whom God has raised from the dead, an event to which they can bear witness. The authorities are distressed that Peter and John should be preaching this message that in Jesus there is resurrection of the dead. They arrest the apostles and put them in prison for the night. Next day Peter and John are brought before the high priest and the council and are asked by what power or by what name they have healed the man. Peter, filled with the Holy Spirit, repeats his straight and uncompromising reply that 'this man is standing before you in good health by the name of Jesus Christ of Nazareth, whom you crucified, whom God raised from the dead' (Acts 4.10).

What an extraordinary change in Peter. This is the Peter who, some weeks ago, hung about on the very edge of the high priest's house, not daring to go in, denying any connection with Jesus of Nazareth. Now he stands boldly before the entire assembly, witnessing to Jesus and the power of the resurrection. No wonder the authorities recognize the apostles' boldness. They send them home, charging them not to speak of the name of Jesus again, although Peter and John refuse to give such an undertaking. The apostles return to their friends and the community to pray and to give thanks for their deliverance. What follows is another dramatic intervention by the Holy Spirit, shaking the foundations of the house where they are gathered, and once again making them bold in their proclamation (Acts 4.31).

Faced with their first real challenge, what do we see? What was emerging as important at Pentecost is still in place. There is openness to the Holy Spirit still – Peter is filled with the Spirit as he addresses the council and the whole community experiences a fresh outpouring of the Spirit after the apostles' release. There is bold witness to the resurrection – the lame man is raised and both the crowd and the council are told that it has been done in the name of Jesus, crucified and risen. The community has remained strong – in fact after this event there are new converts day by day (Acts 4.47) – and prayer remains at the heart of its life. Something new has also become part of the apostolic life. Peter and John begin to share Jesus' ministry of healing. The man at the Beautiful Gate is but the beginning of it. More will follow.

Peter is modelling the life of the mature disciple – open to the Spirit, witnessing to the resurrection, living in community, faithful in prayer, sharing Jesus' work of bringing healing. Peter is looking like God's friend. Most of those who want to follow Jesus will feel, most of the time, that they fall a long way short of that mature discipleship. But even for Peter this has not been an instant embrace of the way of Jesus. It has been a long journey from the first 'Follow me' – and even now, there are still moments when the old Peter, who does not understand and says precisely the wrong thing, comes to the fore.

8

There is nothing unclean

The new, confident Peter who is exercising leadership in the young church still has new experiences to undergo and new things to learn. Such is the way with followers of Jesus, for God always has surprises. Peter now comes to the city of Joppa. Here there will be two new developments in his discipleship. We are informed of the first quite briefly and with no great drama: Peter can raise the dead. A disciple called Tabitha, known for her good works and her charity, has died. Peter is sent for and, when he arrives, goes upstairs where Tabitha's body lies. The widows are there weeping. They want to show Peter the tunics and other clothes Tabitha has made. But Peter sends them all out before kneeling, praying and then addressing the lifeless body. 'Tabitha, get up,' he says. And she does. She opens her eyes and he helps her up (Acts 9.38–41a).

Peter is now doing what Jesus did. The story is, of course, reminiscent of Jesus' raising of the daughter of the leader of the synagogue (Luke 8.41–56). Peter was one of the witnesses to that miracle when Jesus, having come to the leader's house, sent the people out of the room and called upon the one who was dead to get up. Now we have further evidence that the work of God in bringing to life did not stop with the resurrection of Jesus Christ. It is God's nature to raise up. That's a lesson the follower of Jesus has to go on learning. Christian faith commits us to relationship with a God who is always raising up. With the eyes of faith, we can see it all around us, and looking into our mind and heart we can see it happening within our own lives too.

The raising of Tabitha has brought Peter to Joppa, where he stays with Simon, a tanner, and he is now well placed for an extraordinarily important event that marks one of the huge shifts in the life of the early Christian community, with Peter at the very centre of it. The story is told three times, once in the narrative of Acts by Luke, its author, twice by Peter defending himself against his critics. In Caesarea there is a centurion, Cornelius, a devout and generous man; not a Jew, he is therefore described by Jews as a 'Gentile', an outsider. Cornelius has had a vision telling him to send to Joppa and ask for Simon Peter. Meanwhile Peter, up on the roof and at prayer, is also having a vision. He is hungry too – food is on his mind. He falls into some kind of trance:

> He saw the heaven opened and something like a large sheet coming down, being lowered to the ground by its four corners. In it were all kinds of four-footed creatures and reptiles and birds of the air. Then he heard a voice saying, 'Get up, Peter; kill and eat.' But Peter said, 'By no means, Lord; for I have never eaten anything that is profane or unclean.' The voice said to him again, a second time, 'What God has made clean, you must not call profane.' This happened three times, and the thing was suddenly taken up to heaven. (Acts 10.11–16)

It is while he is trying to make sense of what must have been for him an extraordinary and challenging vision that the people whom Cornelius has sent arrive seeking Peter out. Peter who has denied three times, Peter who has been restored to friendship with Jesus three times, is now facing a new challenge. Is the good news of Jesus simply for the Jews, or is it for everyone? Once again God speaks to him through a question repeated three times, signifying that this is one of those transform-ational moments. 'Peter, will you get up and kill and eat?' 'No, Lord, nothing unclean has ever entered my mouth.' 'What God has made clean, you must not call profane.' And then a second time, 'Peter, will you get up and kill and eat?' 'No, Lord, nothing unclean has ever entered my mouth.' 'What God has made clean, you must not call profane.' And a third time: 'Peter, will you get up and kill and eat?' 'No, Lord, nothing unclean has ever entered my mouth.' 'What God has made clean, you must not call profane.' As he puzzled over the vision, Peter may have remembered what Jesus said to him when he had washed his feet. 'One who has bathed does not need to wash, except for the feet, but is entirely clean. And you are clean' (John 13.10).

Peter receives the men sent by Cornelius, listens to their story and invites them in to stay (that in itself is the crossing of a significant boundary); next day, he goes with them to Caesarea and to the home of Cornelius and his family. Peter has to make sense of the truth that, because of the utterly unshakeable love of God that took Jesus to the cross, all that is unclean, profane, soiled, is cleansed. Nothing, nobody, is unclean, for the love of God has wiped away all stains. Peter knows it in his own life. Jesus did this wonderfully for him; he is utterly repentant, restored to his mutual love with Jesus. And now he needs to know that the same unconditional cleansing love is available to all, just as it was to him.

Peter engages with Cornelius, listens to his story and tells those present the good news of Jesus. He speaks of the Holy Spirit and of the death and resurrection of Jesus. It is the message he always preaches, but this time it is to a Gentile household. The outcome is, of course, no surprise to us, though it astounded the Jews who were Peter's companions. As Peter speaks, the Holy Spirit comes upon Cornelius and his family, they speak in tongues and Peter baptizes them (Acts 10.44–48).

When, back in Jerusalem, he tells the story to those who have been criticizing him, their response – for he has won them over – is to play back to him a truth from his own life that is now to be shared with all whom the Lord calls. Peter says to them:

> 'I remembered the word of the Lord, how he had said, "John baptized with water, but you will be baptized with the Holy Spirit." If then God gave them the same gift that he gave us when we believed in the Lord Jesus Christ, who was I that I could hinder God?' When they heard this they were silenced. And they praised God, saying, 'Then God has given even to the Gentiles the repentance that leads to life.'   (Acts 11.16–18)

'God has given to the Gentiles the repentance that leads to life' – Peter knew all about 'the repentance that leads to life', from the moment he wept bitterly at what he had done in denying Jesus till that moment when Jesus asked him three times if he loved him and gave him care of the sheep. And now he had been given the privilege of sharing the good news about the repentance that leads to life with others.

And when these critics in Jerusalem responded to Peter, recognizing that God had been at work in him, they praised God. The word translated 'praise' at that point is the same word used by Jesus at the supper – 'glorified'. They glorified God, for in the drawing of the Gentiles into the church they were seeing again the intimate love of Jesus and, behind it, the intimate love of God.

For Peter this experience has brought him back to some of the key moments in his own journey, maybe to the foot-washing, maybe to the three moments of denial and the three moments of restoration. It has faced him with a major new dimension to faith, over which he has had to puzzle and pray, and from which he has learned about a broader inclusion – a wideness in God's mercy that he had not previously understood.

Being a disciple of Jesus Christ is never about joining an exclusive sect, always about the desire to embrace the whole of humanity. It is not only Peter who has to learn this. In a sense Peter had to learn it first so that the whole community might absorb it soon after – as it did when Peter defended his action once again at the Jerusalem Council (Acts 15.1–11) and paved the way for Paul to defend his own action in going to the Gentiles. It is a message the Church has to go on learning – the amazing wideness of God's mercy.

For the would-be follower of Jesus it is really important to hear and heed this message. It is sometimes difficult to experience it in the Church, or at least in particular local church communities, for they can seem to be companies of the like-minded. They attract people similar to themselves. In their better moments they want to break out of that narrowness, but some of the time they quite like the cosiness of a club where nothing will be too challenging. That is simply not good enough for a disciple of Jesus Christ; nor does such a church reflect the variety of the motley crew of disciples who went about with Jesus, let alone the diversity that developed when the church escaped from the constraints of Judaism. A true follower of Jesus will, like Peter, learn inclusivity and then work to bring it about, defending it, if necessary, as Peter did before the Jerusalem Council.

The pressing issues in the Church today are not about Jew and Gentile, though in some parts of the world nationality and ethnicity are still relevant. More common in western culture is exclusion on grounds of sexual orientation, whether of gay, lesbian, bisexual or transgender people. However much debate there is in the Church about sexual ethics (and the Church is not very good at having open and honest debate about this), welcome and inclusion of all people sincerely seeking the friendship of God should never be in doubt. Women, too, undoubtedly experience more exclusion from the fellowship of the Church, and certainly from ministry, than most would want to face, and that is not simply about whether women should be ordained as bishops. There are also communities where the colour of a person's skin can still lead to exclusion, however subtly it comes about. It would be good to be able to say that, just as the issue is no longer about Jew and Gentile, nor is it about ideas of cleanness and uncleanness, such as Peter struggled with. But the truth is that that sort of prejudice still lurks just below the surface.

The attitudes they sometimes find there can tempt new disciples of Jesus to walk away from the institutional Church. Peter's story is an encouragement to stay, because it witnesses both to how a person can change and also to how, having changed, that person can work to change the institution, as Peter so successfully did. Sometimes a disciple needs to turn into a prophet, say unpalatable things, protest against prejudice and injustice – even break the rules, as Peter did. For Peter's most significant act, long before he defended his action in Jerusalem, before even he baptized Cornelius and his family in Joppa, was to cross a boundary. Simply by responding to the request to go to Cornelius's house, he entered a new world. Crossing boundaries to meet the excluded is surely what a disciple of Jesus does.

From the moment that Peter makes this extraordinary breakthrough in the home of Cornelius, the focus in Acts is much more on Paul, the one who became most obviously the 'apostle of the Gentiles'. Yet there is a more fascinating, beautiful and significant story of Peter in Acts before his ministry is entirely eclipsed, in that book, by Paul. Told in Acts 12, it is another of those occasions when the God of surprises does something unexpected. It may not tell us anything new about Peter and about becoming God's friend, but it underlines truths that have already emerged. It is important also for being the last story of Peter in the pages of Scripture and one that recapitulates much of what has gone before.

King Herod has arrested James, one of the three intimates described in the Gospels, and has summarily put him to death, the first of the 12 to die for his faith. The opponents of the new Christian movement are particularly pleased at this, for James has been killed by beheading, regarded as a particularly ignominious form of death reserved for those who apostatized and adopted a false religion. Seeing that it was a popular move, Herod decides to do the same with Peter, who is in real danger of losing his life. Peter is in prison awaiting some kind of trial, while the community prays fervently for him. The night before his trial, when Peter is asleep, chained and guarded, an angel appears, fills his cell with light, wakes him and urges him to come. His chains fall off and he puts on his belt, his cloak and his sandals and follows the angel. Past two sets of guards they go and through the prison gate that miraculously opens to them. At this stage Peter cannot believe this is real; surely it's just a dream. But once outside, the angel having disappeared, he comes to his senses, realizes that it really is happening to him and exclaims, 'Now I am sure that the Lord has sent his angel and rescued me from the hands of Herod and from all that the Jewish people were expecting' (Acts 12.6–11).

The story has echoes of the Passion and resurrection of Jesus. It takes place during the Feast of Unleavened Bread, at the time of Passover. A King Herod (though a different one) has a role in the event. Like Jesus, Peter is handed over to the soldiers. As at the empty tomb the stone was rolled away, here the prison doors open of their own accord. There the women were startled by angels, here Peter is surprised by the sudden appearance of the angel. Later Peter will have an encounter with a maid-servant in the courtyard, just as he did on the night of Jesus' arrest. This time, though, we know her name, Rhoda: she hears his knock, opens the door and is filled with joy, but leaves Peter standing outside as she rushes off to tell the others who are still praying for him.

> They said to her, 'You are out of your mind!' But she insisted it was so. They said, 'It is his angel.' Meanwhile Peter continued knocking; and when they opened the gate, they saw him and were amazed. He motioned to them with his hand to be silent, and described for them how the Lord had brought him out of prison. And he added, 'Tell this to James and to the believers.' Then he left and went to another place.   (Acts 12.15–17)

The response of the people in the house – 'You are out of your mind!' – corresponds with the response of the 11 to the message of the women concerning Jesus' empty tomb: 'These words seemed to them an idle tale, and they did not believe them' (Luke 24.11). On that occasion it was Peter himself who got up to investigate. At the resurrection, they thought Jesus was a ghost; here they believe Peter is an angel. Finally, with the gate opened, Peter enters the house, to their amazement, a response parallel to that of the disciples encountering the Risen Lord. But, as with Jesus, when he has spoken with them, Peter withdraws and goes to another place.

Other than the words he speaks at the Jerusalem Council, where he recapitulates his experience in the house of Cornelius, this is where the story of Peter stops as far as Scripture is concerned. It is a good place to stop, because it reveals a Peter who is indeed following in the footsteps of Jesus, reliving something of the Passion and the resurrection that, because of his denial and his restoration, means so much to him; a Peter who is beginning to be conformed not only to the life of Jesus, but to his death, though we need to go outside Scripture to learn how that came to completion. It reveals a Peter who has grown confident and courageous in faith, close to Jesus and open to God. His escape from prison becomes a demonstration that the resurrection of Jesus will continue to empower the apostolic Church. The power of the resurrection can be seen in Peter. It will be seen in other disciples too.

Being 'conformed to Christ' may be the work of a lifetime. It happens slowly and gradually. Even those who come to faith suddenly and dramatically cannot hurry this process. As in Peter, it takes time. It is partly a matter of consciously seeking to model our life on that of Jesus. Although it is a matter of grace, it is something nevertheless that we have to work at. We do so by exploring the life of Jesus – especially the key events of it, and supremely the days leading to his death and resurrection – and by reliving his experiences. That's a large part of what the festivals and seasons of the Christian year are about. We relive his experiences with such attention and intensity that we are able to get into his mind and begin to respond to events in a Christ-like way. This is what happened to Peter. And then we find that this pattern has begun to take root. Now it is not so much that we have to work at responding in the way Jesus responded, but that his pattern is being reproduced in us and is beginning to shape our responses. That is being conformed to Christ. It is the work of the Holy Spirit.

In the story with which this chapter began, when Peter raised Tabitha from death, he found himself working in a situation full of echoes of the raising of the daughter of Jairus by Jesus. In the story with which the chapter ends, when he escapes from prison, he finds himself replicating elements of the escape of Jesus from the prison of death. Whatever actually happened on these two occasions, the stories are there to tell us that, if we become disciples of Jesus, increasingly our experiences will be like his as we allow our life and experience to be shaped by him.

9

A drowning man restored to life

There are two books of Christian Scripture that bear the name of Peter. One, known as the First Letter of Peter, begins, 'Peter, an apostle of Jesus Christ, to the exiles of the Dispersion' (1 Peter 1.1); the other, known as the Second Letter of Peter, begins 'Simeon Peter, a servant and apostle of Jesus Christ' and is addressed to 'those who have received a faith as precious as ours through the righteousness of God and of Jesus our Lord' (2 Peter 1.1).

It is worth exploring these two letters, because they reveal to us an older Peter, looking back on the years of his discipleship and his friendship with Jesus when his life is nearing its end. What has he learned? And therefore what can we learn as we explore the insights of the older Peter?

For most of Christian history it was assumed that these two letters were the authentic work of Simon Peter, writing, probably from Rome, before his martyr's death around the year 64 CE, or at the very least providing the material for a secretary or scribe. Indeed 1 Peter speaks of Silvanus, through whom 'I have written this short letter'. In truth the apostle's authorship is very unlikely. The literary style is not that of a Galilean fisherman and the references to church life suggest a later date, when Peter is no longer on the scene. Nevertheless 1 Peter, and less definitely 2 Peter also, come from a date not much later than when Peter would have been writing and almost certainly from the city of Rome where he ended his days. The creators of these letters – in the case of 1 Peter probably soon after 70 CE, and definitely before the end of the century – knew Peter and were part of the church in Rome. Scholars refer to this group as the Petrine circle. Many of them not only knew Peter, but were no doubt witness to his later ministry and possibly to his death, and would have absorbed his teaching. These are complex writings: 1 Peter is theologically very rich, 2 Peter is challenging. In this chapter we cannot begin to engage with all the themes of the letters, but simply to look for what resonates with what we know already about Peter.

The purpose of 1 Peter is 'to encourage you and to testify that this is the true grace of God' and, the writer adds, 'stand fast in it' (5.12). 2 Peter is intended to have something of the character of a last will and testament:

> I think it right, as long as I am in this body, to refresh your memory, since I know that my death will come soon, as indeed our Lord Jesus Christ has made clear to me. And I will make every effort so that after my departure you may be able at any time to recall these things.   (2 Peter 1.13–15)

There is the authentic ring in this passage of an old man nearing his end. Perhaps Peter's circle did recall his desire, nearing his death, to refresh their memory about the things that really mattered. The NRSV translation hides how delightfully, in the original Greek, the writer describes this life and future death. He does not speak of being 'in this body', but 'in this tent'; not of his death, but of the 'putting off of my tent'. It is a wonderful description of the transitory nature of life on this earth, where the body is a temporary home and life a kind of pilgrimage under canvas. It is quite an insight into the nature of our human existence. The words 'our Lord Jesus Christ has made clear to me' sound as if they come from one who lives in such communion with his Lord that making things clear is something that Jesus does simply as part of an ongoing spiritual relationship. This sounds like the Peter who has become God's friend.

Here in these letters we hear resonances of the Peter we have met in the Gospels and in the Acts of the Apostles. From a Peter who, in Acts, was so often filled with the Spirit and saw the Spirit come upon new Christians, there is recognition here of the good news that the prophets brought 'by the Holy Spirit sent from heaven, because no prophecy ever came by human will, but men and women moved by the Holy Spirit spoke from God' (1 Peter 1.12; 2 Peter 1.21). From one who at Caesarea Philippi recognized Jesus as the Christ, the Son of the living God, comes the affirmation that Christ 'was destined before the foundation of the world, but revealed at the end of the ages for your sake' (1 Peter 1.20), so that we 'may become participants of the divine nature' (2 Peter 1.4). From the one who strayed, but was later commissioned to care for the sheep and tend the lambs, comes the reassurance that, although 'you were going astray like sheep, you have now returned to the shepherd and guardian of your souls' (1 Peter 2.25). From the one who was called by Jesus the rock, but was also called a stumbling-block, there is joy in Jesus as a living and precious cornerstone, but one that makes the disobedient stumble, 'a rock that makes them fall' (1 Peter 2.6–8). From the one who learned from a master, who called him friend, what it meant truly to be a servant, comes a letter from 'Simeon Peter, a servant' (literally 'a slave') 'and apostle of Jesus Christ' (2 Peter 1.1). From one who denied his Lord come the words about false teachers who 'will even deny the Master who bought them' (2 Peter 2.1).

After its opening greeting, 1 Peter starts with one of the great purple passages of the New Testament (1.3–9). 'Blessed be the God and Father of our Lord Jesus Christ! By his great mercy he has given us a new birth into a living hope through the resurrection of Jesus Christ from the dead,' it begins. There is so much of Peter in this passage – the sense of new birth, of a fresh start, both in his calling to follow as a disciple and in his calling again to follow after Jesus has been raised, the emphasis on the resurrection that comes through so clearly in Acts. He goes on to speak of the testing of faith: 'for a little while you have had to suffer various trials, so that the genuineness of your faith, being more precious than gold that, though perishable, is tested by fire, may be found to result in praise and glory and honour'. Peter probably knows that more testing of faith awaits him. Indeed. Jesus warned him of it many years ago, at the end of the conversation by the lakeside (John 21.18–19). He speaks also of love for Jesus, for 'although you have not seen him, you love him'. The whole seven-verse passage is a great outpouring of praise, a single long sentence packed with one theological theme after another, but held together by gratitude to a gracious God, the Father of Jesus Christ. The First Letter of Peter sets all these themes out at the beginning and then expands on them in the chapters that follow.

We need to look at two of these themes now, for they reinforce the way of the disciple. A third, relating to suffering, will wait till our final chapter. The first is about relationship with Jesus. How does the disciple relate to Jesus? The overwhelming answer has to be through loving him.

Peter has been schooled by Jesus in the language of love. Jesus revealed his love for his disciples in the washing of their feet on the night before he died, and taught them there and then that this loving action was one they were to do for one another, pressing the message home as he talked about love and gave them a new commandment. Mutual love was to mark their calling and their common life. For Peter, in particular, there was also the lesson to be learned that the love for the community flows from a primary love for the Lord. Three times Peter responded to the invitation to say that he loved Jesus and three times he affirmed that he was his loving friend. Now what does the First Letter of Peter have to say on the matter?

First of all, of course, it spells out the importance of love within the Christian community. Christians are to 'greet one another with a kiss of love' (5.14). 'Have genuine mutual love, love one another deeply from the heart,' 1 Peter says, 'have unity of spirit, sympathy, love for one another, a tender heart, and a humble mind' (1.22; 3.8). We are above all to 'maintain constant love for one another, for love covers a multitude of sins' (4.8). We would expect no less. But the most striking phrase is in that opening outburst of praise. 'Although you have not seen him, you love him' (1.8) is an assertion about loving Jesus. As such it is unique in Scripture. Often we are urged to love God, our neighbours, certainly husbands and wives, even our enemies, sometimes ourselves, but here someone in Peter's circle has realized that, if Peter's name is on the letter, love for Jesus needs to be expressed. For that – his love for Jesus – is the basis of Peter's apostolic ministry. Paul teaches that anyone who has no love for the Lord should be accursed (1 Corinthians 16.21), but only here in Scripture is it specifically asserted that we should love Jesus and that indeed, although we have not seen him, we do love him.

This is really important for those called into discipleship today. For some it is easy. For them Jesus is the human face of God, attractive and attracting, as he was to Peter by the shore of the lake when he first became a disciple. He made God real for Peter so that a little later, Peter could say of Jesus that he was the Son of the living God. For such people loving Jesus is the most natural thing in the world – they find it much easier to love Jesus, whom they feel they can almost see and touch through the stories the Gospels tell. But it is not like that for everybody. Jesus can seem trapped in a first-century setting, belonging to a biblical era, living in a culture very different from our own, and we know that the Gospel accounts leave all sorts of questions unanswered. It is something to do with our personality, but some of us more readily relate to – love even – the eternal God of mystery and beauty, beyond our comprehension. We may be grateful for what we have learned of this God through the life and death of Jesus, not least that this God of mystery and beauty is a trinity of love overflowing into the world and into human hearts. But somehow we want to bypass Jesus and relate to the mystery. But what the life of Peter says, and what this key line in 1 Peter says, is that you cannot bypass Jesus. You have to fall in love with Jesus. And, if you don't find that happening almost despite yourself, you have to work at it. If Jesus is, as he said to Thomas, 'the way, and the truth, and the life' (John 14.6), he is the way to love, the way to love God and the way to love all those others we are to love – neighbours, family, enemies, ourselves. For all that it is good if we can, like Peter, make some great statement of faith about who this Jesus is, it's not as important as falling in love with him.

How is this loving to happen? There has to be room for intimacy. Peter discovered that both in the upstairs room on a Thursday night before the supper and again on the lakeside after the breakfast at Easter. The Second Letter of Peter recalls that wonderful moment of ecstatic, beautiful intimacy on the mountain of Transfiguration – it was really an intimacy between Jesus and his Father, but he had admitted his friends, Peter among them, into the experience.

We had been eyewitnesses of his majesty. For he received honour and glory from God the Father when that voice was conveyed to him by the Majestic Glory, saying, 'This is my Son, my Beloved, with whom I am well pleased.' We ourselves heard this voice come from heaven, while we were with him on the holy mountain. (2 Peter 1.16b–19)

Loving is expressed through intimacy. It is also expressed through following. By the time these letters were written, following always meant taking up the cross and following; it was an age of persecution. Not always physical persecution, though there was that, but always verbal persecution, a kind of sneering derisory dismissal of the faith of the Christian. Disciples are to handle it the way Jesus handled suffering. 'To this you have been called,' 1 Peter says, 'because Christ also suffered for you, leaving you an example, so that you should follow in his steps' (2.20–21).

Following in the steps of Jesus is always part of the disciple's call. The younger Peter knew that. But there is also something else, which perhaps only comes with time. It is a new word in the shaping of the life of the disciple and a word that has the same root as 'disciple'. The word is 'discipline'. Peter uses it three times (1 Peter 1.13; 4.7; 5.8). The word in the Greek is *nephontes* and can be translated 'self-controlled' or 'sober-minded'. Followers of Jesus are to 'prepare your minds for action' (literally, 'gird up the loins of the mind') and to 'discipline yourselves; set all your hope on the grace that Jesus Christ will bring you when he is revealed' (1.13).

Somewhere along the line, those trying to follow the way of Jesus find the need for a discipline, a rule or rhythm of life, that will keep them close to Jesus and enable them to work patiently at the holiness to which they are called. For some this is simply an individual pattern, perhaps worked out with a spiritual director or 'soul friend'. For others it means committing to a communal rule in some kind of community or fellowship, whether an attachment to a traditional religious community of monks, friars or sisters or one of the new kinds of community in the fresh expressions of church where there is increasing engagement with what is being called 'the new monasticism'. People are being helped by a personal rule, one not imposed by an outside authority but accepted voluntarily and drawn up with the individual personality in mind, about that person's prayer life, study of Scripture, social and personal relationships, use of money, care for the earth's resources. A disciple will not get very far without a discipline. Peter is clear about that. It is a way to 'grow in the grace and knowledge of our Lord and Saviour Jesus Christ' (2 Peter 3.18), a way of living in his friendship.

The second theme is the great Petrine theme of resurrection. Peter had run to the tomb of Jesus, had met the Risen Lord, had been restored by him, had preached the resurrection and had raised the dead in a way that reflected the ministry of Jesus. Now in the burst of praise with which the First Letter of Peter begins we have a strong affirmation of the power of the resurrection: 'By his great mercy he has given us a new birth into a living hope through the resurrection of Jesus Christ from the dead' (1 Peter 1.3).

But what happens in these letters is that something implicit in the Gospels and in Peter's experience is made explicit. It is the relationship between the resurrection and baptism. We have noted already the baptismal undertone of what happened when Peter was saved by Jesus as he failed to walk on the water. There was the foot-washing in John 13 with its baptismal associations. Peter called on his hearers to be baptized and himself baptized Gentiles as well as Jews. But now 1 Peter spells it out. Speaking of Jesus, the letter asserts:

He was put to death in the flesh, but made alive in the spirit, in which also he went and made a proclamation to the spirits in prison, who in former times did not obey, when God waited patiently in the days of Noah, during the building of the ark, in which a few, that is, eight people, were saved through water. And baptism, which this prefigured, now saves you – not as a removal of dirt from the body, but as an appeal to God for a good conscience, through the resurrection of Jesus Christ.

(1 Peter 3.18b–21)

The 'appeal to God for a good conscience through the resurrection of Jesus Christ' seems at first an odd definition of what baptism achieves, but there are the beginnings here, in what seems like the first articulation of baptismal theology, of an understanding of the link between baptism and resurrection that Paul spells out in Romans 6, when he asks whether his readers realize that everyone who has been baptized has been baptized into the death of Christ.

We have been buried with him by baptism into death, so that, just as Christ was raised from the dead by the glory of the Father, so we too might walk in newness of life.

For if we have been united with him in a death like his, we will certainly be united with him in a resurrection like his.

(Romans 6.4–5)

In the more settled Christian society of the last millennium, most people were brought to baptism by their parents before they were old enough to remember it. There might have been opportunities in later life to reclaim one's baptism, as there still are, but for most people there was no time to decide that this was the right occasion to take the step that most clearly signalled an acceptance of Christ's subversive pattern of life out of death. It is different now. Many find their way into faith before baptism, perhaps hardly knowing about baptism, perhaps sharing in the bread and wine the Church blesses and shares at the table, before discovering the font and with it a moment where a decision has to be made. It is a big step, but one that brings much blessing, to identify with Jesus who went down into the water of the Jordan and later went also through the deep waters of death on a journey to resurrection, and with Peter, the drowning man whom Jesus raised up and drew into new life. Whether we look back to something that happened in the past or look to it as something that lies ahead of us, it is a big step and a blessing. The reference in 1 Peter to Noah and the ark suggests it is all the more so for those, like Peter himself, who have been through hell.

For me, knowing myself to be one of the baptized, a member of the baptismal community, has always been important. The way I often explain its significance is to make the distinction between the phrase 'I was baptized', something people will often say in order to tell you about an event, often one that happened long ago (in my own case when I was seven weeks old), and 'I am baptized', in the present tense, reinforcing that my baptism has committed me to a particular lifestyle in following Jesus. It makes my baptism, and my reflection on it, a significant factor in my ongoing Christian formation. My status as one of the baptized shapes the process of being conformed to Christ, of which I wrote in the last chapter. As a bishop it is one of my chief joys to baptize and it is more often adults that I baptize than children. Standing with candidates at the font, inviting them to affirm their faith, pouring the water over them, anointing them with the holy oil, putting an arm around them in an embrace of welcome is a huge privilege. There is, as I wrote in relation to Peter and the quasi-baptismal experience of being rescued by Jesus from the water as a drowning man, a right moment in any Christian life to take this step or to reclaim in adult life something done in infancy, and no one can prescribe when it ought to be. There needs to be an inner conviction. But that moment when it comes is a moment of joy. How often I have seen that joy written on the faces of those who come to baptism. When earlier in life they have been through some kind of hell, as had Peter, it is all the more sheer joy.

10

You will stretch out your hands

We last heard of Peter when he was in Jerusalem to attend the council that decisively opened the Christian community to the Gentiles. This took place around the year 50 CE. At some point he was in Antioch and he may well have been in Corinth at another point. But the likelihood is that before very long he found his way to Rome. As we have noted, the letters that bear his name seem very likely to have come from Rome, and to have been shaped by Peter's circle and influenced by the reflections of the apostle himself. They are, of course, letters written to suffering Christians. We need to stop and explore this theme of suffering now, not only because it enables us to understand something of how Peter approached his own final time of trial, but because following Jesus can – sometimes ought to – involve suffering. 'Take up your cross and follow' is sometimes real enough, whether the suffering entails the bearing of physical pain or verbal ridicule or, just occasionally, something infinitely more testing. Becoming part of the Christian community can also expose you to the abuse sometimes received by the Church, justly sometimes, no doubt, when it behaves foolishly, but more often for its defence of gospel values.

The First Letter of Peter is overwhelmingly about suffering, how it is to be both interpreted and embraced and how the community must not be surprised by it:

Beloved, do not be surprised at the fiery ordeal that is taking place among you to test you, as though something strange were happening to you. But rejoice insofar as you are sharing Christ's sufferings, so that you may also be glad and shout for joy when his glory is revealed. (1 Peter 4.12–14)

Suffering here seems to be in part about being misunderstood and ridiculed, perhaps more than about physical abuse. You might wonder whether 'the fiery ordeal' in verse 12 represents real persecution, physical danger, but scholars think that it is a reference simply to the uncertainties of the last days. This is a community that is ridiculed and reviled, its members thought to be misfits, rather than one being brought before the authorities or thrown to the lions. And patient faithfulness is probably more difficult in the face of ridicule than life-threatening persecution. For the newly baptized, as many of the letter's readers presumably were – Peter speaks of 'newborn infants' (1 Peter 2.1) – the temptation to abandon the faith under the pressure to conform must have been huge. What they are being asked to do is to preserve their Christian distinctiveness and to stand out from the surrounding culture. This has a very contemporary resonance. While in parts of Africa and Asia, Christians live with the real possibility of martyrdom, in the West ridicule rather than violent persecution is the weapon with which the Church is undermined. For someone trying to be a follower of Jesus today, the constant insidious attack, not on individual Christians, but on the truth of the faith itself, is a painful matter.

Although there may not have been widespread physical persecution of Christians at this particular time – that was to come later – there were outbreaks of violent action. Stephen, the first Christian martyr, had died for the faith (Acts 7.58–60), stoned to death, and James, one of the three intimates of Jesus, had been executed by Herod (Acts 12.1–2). Peter, as we have noted, had had a lucky escape through divine intervention.

There were sporadic outbursts of serious physical persecution – imprisonment and sentence to death – in Rome, especially in the reign of Nero from 54 to 68 CE. It is during this period, and probably in 64 CE, that Peter was imprisoned and put to death. For Peter, of course, to suffer was to fulfil his calling to take up the cross and follow. Following in the footsteps of Jesus, responding to his example, was exactly what he was committed to doing and exactly what Jesus had assured him he would do.

What do we know of the circumstances of Peter's death? There is no contemporary document, though the Fourth Gospel indicates that it knows the manner of his death – 'he said this to indicate the kind of death by which he would glorify God' (John 21.19) – as if it were written after an event of which the early Church was well aware. There is a good deal of information from the second and third centuries. The apocryphal *Acts of Peter*, a second-century document, tells the story of how Peter was persuaded to leave Rome by the church there to avoid arrest, but, in a vision, met Jesus going into the city. 'Lord, where are you going?' Peter asked. Jesus replied, 'I am going to Rome to be crucified again.' Peter, determined not to let down his master again, turned back to face arrest and martyrdom.

Reliable Christian writers in the second and third centuries fill in some of the details. He was confined in the Mamertine prison and then taken to the gardens of Nero, a frequent place of execution, and put to death by crucifixion, head downward at his own request, because he was not worthy to die just like his master. His body was interred in the Tropaion, a memorial shrine in a cemetery on the Vatican Hill.

It was to this martyr's death, in which it seems certain that he was followed soon after by Paul, that Jesus was pointing in that extraordinary conversation some thirty years before, when Peter received his commission to tend the flock of Christ. Just as at Caesarea Philippi, Jesus had no sooner confirmed that his vocation was to be the Messiah than he went on to predict his Passion, now, in his conversation with Peter, he no sooner confirmed Peter's vocation to tend the sheep than he went on to predict Peter's own passion. He introduced it with the phrase, 'Very truly' (literally 'Amen, amen'), which in the Fourth Gospel always indicates that a statement of deep significance is to follow.

> 'Very truly, I tell you, when you were younger, you used to fasten your own belt and to go wherever you wished. But when you grow old, you will stretch out your hands, and someone else will fasten a belt around you and take you where you do not wish to go.' (He said this to indicate the kind of death by which he would glorify God.) After this he said to him, 'Follow me.' (John 21.18–19)

Death by crucifixion is what Jesus was pointing to, and that is what Peter experienced, firm in his love for Jesus, strong as a friend of God, stretching out his hands just as Jesus had done on the cross, just as the Father does when welcoming home those who return, in the story Jesus told of the return of the prodigal son to his compassionate father.

Here we need to recall for a moment John's detail that Peter, discovering during the fishing expedition that Jesus was on the shore, covered his nakedness before plunging into the sea to come to him. For, all those years later in Rome, facing his martyrdom, he would have hung upon his cross, just as Jesus had done, vulnerable and naked. Only Christian respectability includes a loincloth for those being crucified. Beyond the figure of Peter and beyond the figure of Jesus we see, of course, the vulnerability of God, who for love of our human race emptied himself of divinity to become our brother and our friend and gave his life that the fall from grace of Adam and Eve might be reversed and the denial of Peter, the sinful man, be forgiven.

* * *

That is how it all began, at least as Luke tells it, when Peter found himself responding to Jesus after a miraculous catch of fish. 'Go away from me, Lord, for I am a sinful man,' he said, but, far from going away, or letting Peter go away, Jesus held on to Peter; Peter followed him (Luke 5.9–11). Whether in that way, whether simply because of the unexpected pull of Jesus, or because his brother told him he had found the Messiah, Peter became a follower. Gradually, little by little, as he stayed with Jesus, learned from Jesus, followed as faithfully as he could, tried to be like Jesus, the follower became a disciple. His life began to take on the shape of Jesus' life, his mind started to be conformed to Jesus' mind.

It was slow and there were setbacks. And then Jesus wanted to move it on and to build on his relationship with him as follower and disciple. 'You are my friends,' he said to them. Peter, once he understood that, wanted it so much, but it all went wrong so quickly. Friendship had had no time to establish itself before he had abandoned discipleship and walked away, following no longer, in an act of denial that felt like betrayal. But then, on the day that probably mattered more than any other in his life, he had had the chance to recover it all, to assure Jesus of his friendship, to accept again the love of Jesus. From that moment the friendship held. He was a follower again and a disciple and, by the power of the Holy Spirit at Pentecost, and in the strength of his friendship with Jesus, he became other things too. He became an evangelist, one who tells the good news of God as it is revealed by the life of Jesus. He became a witness, speaking of the resurrection of Jesus, giving evidence of it by the transformation of his own life and finally by a faithfulness that had him stretch out his hands on a cross.

Peter is follower, disciple, evangelist, witness, friend; and as such he is exemplar and encourager. But he is also exemplar and encourager by his human weakness, by his frequent failure to understand, by his habit of saying just the wrong thing, by his struggle, even by his denial. We are drawn to him, inspired by him, because in him so much remained for a long time imperfect and unresolved.

The one thing that never seems to falter in the story of Peter is love. The love of Jesus for Peter is never in doubt, but nor is Peter's love for Jesus. Even when Peter says the wrong thing it is out of deep affection. When Peter denies, what makes it so awful is that this is the man whom he loves. This is the man he wants to call his friend.

I can't help wondering whether Samuel Crossman in the seventeenth century had Peter at all in his mind when he wrote his beautiful hymn, 'My song is love unknown'. It captures superbly the relationship of friendship we have been exploring:

> My song is love unknown,
> my Saviour's love to me,
> love to the loveless shown,
> that they might lovely be.
> O, who am I,
> that for my sake
> my Lord should take
> frail fresh, and die?
>
> He came from his blest throne,
> salvation to bestow:
> but men made strange, and none
> the longed-for Christ would know.
> But, O, my friend,
> my friend indeed,

who at my need
his life did spend.

Here might I stay and sing,
no story so divine;
never was love, dear King,
never was grief like thine!
This is my friend,
in whose sweet praise
I all my days
could gladly spend.

This friendship involved – involves – a vulnerable and intimate, yet tough, and ultimately joyful, deeply satisfying love. I guess it can't be perfect in this life, for the enjoyment of friendship with God, though it can begin on earth, is ultimately for heaven, something humbling and beautiful at the heart of a whole series of friendships, which may be more like the dance we call the communion of saints. That brings me back to where I began, with the Church of St Gregory of Nyssa in San Francisco. For there you can see not only Gregory's words about friendship, but, high up in the dome, looking down on the worship that lifts the heart to heaven, the icon of the dancing saints, the friends of God. I don't see the apostle among them, but there is no doubt that, among the multitude that no one can number in the communion of saints, is to be found Simon Peter – the friend of Jesus and, through him, the friend of God.

So let the penultimate word be with Gregory: 'the one thing truly worthwhile is becoming God's friend'. And the last word with Jesus. As he speaks with Peter by the lakeside, having restored him to friendship, he says, not once, but twice, what he said when it all started: 'Follow me.'

That's the invitation. 'Come to the font maybe. Come to the table often. Come, take up the cross one day. But, always, my friend, God's friend, come, follow me.'